Are We Ready For Change

Pankaj K. Singh

DIAMOND BOOKS
www.diamondbook.in

Publisher : **Diamond Pocket Books (P) Ltd.**
X-30, Okhla Industrial Area, Phase-II
New Delhi-110020
Phone : 011-40712200
E-mail : sales@dpb.in
Website : www.diamondbook.in
Edition : 2018
Printed at : Repro Knowledgecast Limited, Thane

Are We Ready For Change

Author – Pankaj K. Singh

Dedication

The book is dedicated to all the Karmyogis and Yogacharyas, due to whose efforts India today is successful in keeping itself tied with the thread of moral values despite the storm of consumerism today.

Introduction

We always keep complaining about many things in our life. Facing many problems and irregularities we often keep pondering over and hoping for the situations to change. We keep presenting the demand of changes in reference to the entire universe. The system we dwell in and work under we obviously see many problems and limitations which we want to change.

In fact the entire universe is constantly changing. Nature itself keeps the universe new, fresh and qualitative through many kinds of changes conducted by it. The situations and systems in our normal life we want to change, are actually generated by us indirectly. This nation, world and the entire universe is just like the way we are. Therefore even if we want to make a change then we ourselves are the unit of the change. We ourselves are the remote control and minute form of the entire universe. The moment we start changing ourselves, this entire universe starts changing from that moment.

In fact humans' mind, body and soul is the small form of this entire universe. Our mind body and soul is itself the minute form of nature and God. This is our moral responsibility that we keep this minute God land clean, pious and shining. Our life values are being shattered due to the storm of the western consumerism today.

For establishing a peaceful life and organised society we need the foundation of moral values. Man cannot be just slave to organs and matters. The Western consumer culture has kept the people slave to the products. What can be bigger insult to human life than this that we remain as slave to the perishable and promptly perishable products along with physical pleasures leaving our self-welfare and spiritual progress.

In today's consumerist age due to the uncontrolled pleasures and unsaturated desires for the matters, our mind, body and soul have been severely polluted, dirty and sick today. They have been covered with the dust of bad-tendencies. We ourselves have to wipe the dust. For this we have to walk on discipline, good-companionship and goodness. In doing so, there are no specific overt difficulties and obstacles also. Whatever problems and obstacles are borne in this reference, they are developing only due to the enemies in the form of bad-culture within us.

We ourselves are the biggest friend and enemy of ourselves in this universe. If we want to do welfare to us, then we have to badly crush the elements of bad culture within us. We should begin this great journey from today itself. This is for sure that as long as the journey of the self-change does not begin, the process of the nation building can also not proceed further.

This book is only a small request and endeavour to direct us towards the spiritualistic philosophy, national thinking and mental revolution. This is often certain that the construction of this country is not possible only through the land of law, constitution and plans. This requires citizen-construction. As a citizen our journey and direction of self-change will only decide the fate of this country and entire society.

– Pankaj K Singh
(Author)
Email - pkstiger@gmail.com
website – www.pankajsingh.com

Preface

The real progress and elevation of this country originally vested in the every citizen of the nation. If we wish the spiritual progress for every individual, then it would require that the individual himself is aware and make intended efforts for doing this. This is also required that the individual keeps trying to change himself constructively.

In the modern world of today human beings' behaviour and thinking has remained direction less and deviated from the main target of life. Each moment he keeps making efforts for his serving his self-interest by hook or crook. In fact there cannot be any bigger interest of an individual than the interest of society. This simple thing cannot be comprehended by people only because his spiritualistic knowledge and self-knowledge do not get elevated.

Today the man has turned into a victim of demerits, bad-culture, evil-propensities and system's defects. Today a human being is walking on the path of falseness due to being addicted to greed. He has dispensed with hard-work and wants maximum mundane pleasures and benefits by walking on a wrong path without making any hard work.

If there is anything in the universe worth changing then that is solely an individual's behaviour itself. The moment this process of citizen-construction and human-construction begins, this world starts changing and walking on the right direction. Each moment we should keep looking at our own behaviour while trying to change it constructively.

Today unfortunately all the paths to show people knowledge and advises are closed. Parents, family, teachers, educational institutions, society and administrative system are not able to provide with the expected guidance to the people. Due to lack of proper knowledge and guidance, the society and civilians are not able to bear with their responsibilities properly.

In the system stuck in financial-organism and money making, the family and the society along with schools and ruling systems are somewhere or the other deviated from their original targets. The task of providing right guidance and moral education and training has got slower. We need to accelerate the speed. This book presents a way to do the introspection in this direction that how we can direct our life on the path of excellence and quality with getting disciplined and committed.

The writer Pankaj K. Singh is sincerely associated with the process of citizen construction on the basis of national values for last two decades. He has provided many projects and services with new direction and pace on the national level. His social and political projects have been certified and result oriented which have gotten thousands of denizens associated with them now. As a sociologist and a volunteer his personality and contribution is praiseworthy. Every citizen of this country must go through this book along with making efforts to bring its values in their behaviour also. For building a capable and disciplined India it is imperative for each Indian to be awaken.

–Sadguru Swatantradev

Contents

1

Think Auspicious, Think Big

Each person should try to get rid of narrow thoughts. The person who keeps trivial and narrow thoughts about himself, that person in fact is a victim of dreadful mental illness. We need to make special efforts to get rid of such mental ailments. One should try to walk with big thought and generous thinking keeping the same subject in mind. This is but obvious that auspicious thoughts do not give birth to negative sentiments like jealousy, hatred, envy, etc. To bring the mind into a healthy state, one should lighten his or her heavenly element within. Each atom of our mind is revived by the heavenly element. There should never be any deed or effort from our side which could bring obstacle into the heavenly path. During studies, thoughts or the practice (Sadhna) if the heart is not firmly controlled then the expected benefit of that is not received. In-auspicious thinking is the result of the mental debility. This destroys the mind's power of working and the energy and enthusiasm starts deteriorating.

The nature keeps inspiring human beings. If we keep following the rules made by the nature only then we can very well give meaning to our life. The nature has provided all kinds resources to the human being. The nature has filled the universe with all kinds of resources and grandeur. Nature has given us that which even cannot be imagined by us. The journey of evolution of humans is only the search of the resources and the history of the exploration of the elements provided by the nature.

The nature has given light in day hours and darkness in the night. The motive behind is this only that the humans should also follow the path of action without expectation on the path of truth without being deviated from pleasure-sorrow, pain-joy, profit-loss. If our life violates the rule made by the nature and if we keep deteriorating the nature for our carnal pleasures from the nature, then this life and the deeds cannot be called auspicious. And such inauspicious deeds will prove to be bringing the fall of human civilization.

In contrast with the laws of nature in our life is full of darkness of illusion, swooning and affection day and night. Every moment while asleep, awake, while doing anything we keep on viewing financial gains and pleasures. We always keep wishing for prosperity, power and many a rights. Money can be a source to help us avail a better life but it is not the aim of life. We need to understand the difference between the means and the attainable. Today, only finance and pleasure has become the song and music of our life. The good deeds, sensitivity, kind consciousness of philanthropy have been vanished from our life. In fact, the wealth is capable and also in-capable.

All the religions of the world teach us that we are all living beings are the part of the same human family. This is shocking this even after knowing the truth we do not see unity in our society. The society is not able to get unified due to the pride and selfishness. The humanity within ourselves have somewhere been vanished. If we are one family, then where is this brotherhood feeling vanished? Due to the same discriminations human beings are losing the substance of their life. We have to save our humanity from this darkness of inequality and discrimination and then bring it to the light of unity. And this light only can be obtained through spiritualism.

In the want of wealth and with ample of money–both the situations create different kinds of violence and mal-culture. With the right combination of both only could the healthy and non-violent society be produced. Collection with the renunciation is an art of living a balanced life. Like both the aspects of a coin, there are two aspects of consciousness of Punya (the goodness earned from good deeds) and sensitivity also–social aspect and spiritual aspect. Both have their separate venues and separate values. When we get disillusioned with matter, that is pure spiritual benefit or say attainment of Punya. A human being is a social being. He keeps receiving many kinds of securities, facilities and help from the society. In this situation returning the proper favour also comes on his part as a social responsibility. We should not always keep taking things from the nature and the society, but we should also try to them something creatively.

Everyone is in the quest of money, instead of searching Guru

We need to move forward on the path of self-consciousness for sake of freedom from mundane pains and obstacles. Actually all beings in the world look for freedom from all pains forever. They want to reach into such a state where there is happiness all around, there should not be any moment of pain in life. For attaining such a state he tries to reach to God. This is a notion in the society that God cannot be achieved without Guru. For this reason human beings start looking for Guru.

Not being able to understand this vanity fair, human beings consider those as complete saint who are good orator based on Vedas and mythological tales and could deliver good discourses, then people make them their Guru. These Gurus cannot take you out from this world to the perennial and imperishable world. For attaining true devotion of God, we should search for such saint who is aware of the Omnipotent. The one who has the complete knowledge, is the only one who could help an individual get rid of this world into his own world of abode reaching where the being never gets back to this world. Actually the real Guru is that who inspire his disciple to walk on the right path.

On the basis of expediency and self-knowledge one should look for a Guru. The way you do not get the destination by walking on a wrong path, same way by just by singing a wrong-doer's praises and proclaiming him as Guru, cannot clear your way to self-welfare. It needs a continuous efforts to keep your memory, consciousness and expediency while walking on the path of religion and spiritualism. We can do right valuation of a person only with a sight which perceives a human being through the vision of knowledge. Superstition and fetishism strengthen only bad deeds and blind-faith. The society needs to be liberated out of such emotions.

The path of self realization, attainment of sense and spiritual progress is very rare. For this one needs constant guidance of a qualified Guru with a right companionship, discipline and free-practice. It is not easy to walk on the path of spiritualism, but if a man starts walking on it with complete devotion and faith, then the power of the universe does help him and he will get the substance of his life. The moment the change will enter in our life, from that moment only our society will start realizing change. If we wish for an ideal society and wish to give a society full of happiness and equality, then we will have to realize the wish to know the truth within us. This curiosity itself goads us to the path of truth and auspiciousity.

All the people are brothers and sisters in reality. There is no difference among them at all. The justice of nature has also been certified by the science and therapeutics. It is human beings' selfishness which is the reason of the differences and estrangements. If this selfishness and ego cease to exist, then the human civilization can realize the motto of Vasudhaiv Kutumbkam in practice. Originally we are all the posterity of God. And our parents and teachers are also a live representation of the same God. Originally we are all the same siblings of the same God. Our parents and elders are also the same way children of God. We are all the minute partial representation of God. All the religions of the world teach us that we all living beings are the part of the same human family. This is shocking this even after knowing the truth we do not see unity in our society. The society is not able to get unified due to the pride and selfishness. The humanity within ourselves have somewhere been vanished. If we are one family, then where is this brotherhood feeling vanished? Due to the same discriminations human beings are losing the substance of their life. We have to save our humanity from this darkness of inequality and discrimination and then bring it to the light of unity. And this light only can be obtained through spiritualism.

If we want to put humanity in humans, then we have to ignite the candle of spiritualism. If a human being closing his eyes try to concentrate in dark, tries to do away with the negativity within and present the will to assimilate within God – then even in darkness he will see the ray of light. That is not just light, it is God within the light in a formless form. The person who could be able to behold that light, will be able to get away with all the jealousy from within. His way of thinking will change. For him every individual will be the same.

If every individual starts walking on the path of spiritualism, then it will bring such a change in the entire world that all the pains and miseries along with all kinds of inequality and crimes of the world would be eloped. All the religions of the world show the path of spiritualism and it is the biggest religion. If we all walk on the path of spirituality it will not only elevate our spiritual life but also promote the life of our society. The change cannot come to one's life just like that in a moment, this is a process. If you keep the Sadhna intact, then after some time you reach to this stage of change.

Every person wants the participation in good deeds along with respect. This is not only his physical but also the inner need. Undoubtedly the human soul is great, and it has its own special glory. Though due to the un-static nature of mind a human being has dimmed the shining of his soul, still this tendency keeps sustaining in his life that he would keep wanting to do some good deeds possible. It gets attracted to this side where it gets respect. We need to live a manner-full life with proper social behaviour. This behaviour and manner full living would give us proper respect. This is not necessary that we are able to help everyone necessarily, it is also not possible to help everyone coming to us for help. On all such occasions we should let our limitation be known to the person. And for this calling him good or bad is also not good. We can also say No, telling the person our helplessness.

In our normal life when someone comes to us with a request for help, we should in fact say thanks to him that he found us worth asking for help. After his arrival without caring about his or her age greeting him or her with Namaste, offering him a chair to sit, and expressing our happiness on his arrival we should ask for his well being – this is a normal mannerism. We should behave like this with everyone that anyone coming to us, we should asked about his or her well being. It is not expensive at all. This is also required for the maintenance of social life. This has a positive impact on the other person. This normal mannerism study becomes a part of our life. Later on, this provides us with lots of peace and benefits as well, especially when we reach to the top of success then the gentleness is truly inevitable. As they say-'the tree full of fruits is naturally little bent.'

2

This body is not the virtual truth

In today's age people have thought their physical bodies as the final truth, being ignorant we take this physical world as the only truth. We have also adapted to this, you may call it utilitarian culture of the West. The bad effect of this is that people have taken the collection of materialistic objects and physical pleasure out of their physical body as the ultimate target of life. The people are trying their hard might be for obtaining this only. They do not even have this much of time to sit and ponder over his behaviour and future life. He is fully involved in the pleasures of this world considering them the best achievement of their lives.

The misconception of considering our physical body as our asset forever, makes us feel that we will also be finished after death. Not only this but due to the incorporation with the body we feel that we are young or middle aged or old whereas if we try to sit with ourselves stopping the horse-run of our mind then we sure will feel the consciousness within us which is the source of all thoughts which is not even young not even old. Our body is different from us and it keeps changing overtly. Consciousness has no age neither does it parish. The information and knowledge together every day get accumulated in our memories. This intellectual upliftment is considered by us as our development. The same way in accordance with the age when we get young or middle aged or old afterwards this perishable body gets perished and we consider this process finally as death.

At the level of normal wisdom we find this as just natural and true. As long as we don't get the claims of that element which is beyond the growth of the body and logics and arguments. Also, there is no way that can ever be perished, we are not able to get out of the perishability of this body. The element of consciousness which is within us is our own absolute power, the realisation of the same feeling right away stops our connection with our body and at the same time the fear of death gradually starts perishing within us. As a truth finally we realise that the death actually is the beginning. This state of mind kills the fear of getting killed or the fear of death. A man can realise the realisation of God only in the state of no fear.

If there is true trust and faith towards God within a human being then he becomes free of all worries. Once he holds this within him that the Almighty is so merciful so benevolent and loving then the bonds of hope and disappointment start breaking. The person starts concentrating himself on his deeds and gets free out of the worries of the results. This encouragement takes him towards the state of an indulgence which is the absolute state of spiritualism. Where a man is free from happiness-grief, respect-disrespect, criticism-admiration. This brings an end to all his astray.

A man should keep his attitude positive and kind. The positive attitude helps him progress. That he comes to know that while living in the society he has to help others as well while expecting their help and this way living with the proximity of others' life is full of natural beauty. The positive attitude keeps a man away from violence, ego, revenge and jealousy. Such person only likes to live peacefully with protection. His vision towards life is without any expectation and full of positivity since the ultimate truth of life positivity and positive relativity. For the growth of positive vision we need to control our inner tendency of selfishness and the same behaviour. Although everybody is selfish up to some extent but that can be controlled by giving it a direction. A person with such vision always care of others' happiness the way he does of his own. Not only this, others also support him in this process this is what is expected by him. This expectation get fulfilled it is not necessary. Positive attitude is the foundation of our life. Positivity brings meaningfulness and simplicity in life. Getting free from anxiety and with strong determination an individual can get full of self confidence and then only he has got the capacity to contribute towards the development of society and self also.

A man has to be fearless and strong to follow the path of truth. After truth and discipline only courage is the best quality of a human being. If we do not even have courage and self power then we are not efficient to do anything. Courage less person neither can do anything for the society nor for himself.

If courage is the name of our body power then positive courage is the name of the power of our soul. We see the lives of all great men in the world full of positive courage and a positive way built out of that. Winning the darkness and marching forward without getting diverted by obstacles and the determination of making impossible into possible is called positive courage.

The people who have courage of embracing death for the sake of society, country and humanity are truly great men. When the sensitivity within us is on high then we are able to defeat illiteracy, crime, violence, inhumanity and torture. When truth and power get mixed then the person's the winner in true sense. When truthfulness like sun does not have his grace in the form of courage then possibly a person can't do anything.

Do not run after physical pleasures blindly

Human being keeps chasing desires and wishes in his lifetime some of the desires get fulfilled but most of them do not. Once his desires are fulfilled he is very happy. Many times he gets highly egoistic and gives all the credit to himself for his success. On the contrary when his desires are not fulfilled then he blamed it on God and his fate. There is no end to the desires, they are limitless. Once one desire get fulfilled then the other one occurs. They keep on coming one after one, and this process is life long.

In today's materialistic world people have more requirements than their limitations. Many times they have such high ambitions which have no basis on the surface of reality. In this perishable world a man is always making efforts for achieving physical places. he always keeps longing for that. He doesn't know that he himself is a form of happiness. Existing under its characteristics this world is perishable. It is going to end, then why should he run after desires? An individual cannot get righteous passage without getting out of desires and ambitions.

As long as our behaviour is not according to nature and consists of moral values till then it will be impossible for us to achieve high spiritualistic state and consciousness. We need to do the introspection on our own behaviour and thought process before anything. When we talked about impractical spiritual things in our life then this spiritualism is like doing injustice to nature. Why is it so because spiritualism arrives after parting ways from this materialistic world. The meaning of spiritualism is not a subject of teaching or learning. It exists in all living beings including human beings. When a man tries to practise observing natural events around him then from the same moment it starts bringing spiritual by feeling in his life.

If men did not wander about in the quest of desires, greed and selfishness then he would not have to live a life based on artificiality. A man should stay away from the greed, consumption and selfishness all the time. He should always stay content with the things he got and he always keep trying to move forward to the freedom forever called Moksha. The man who does not expect many desires in future along with the fear of it he actually is able to enjoy the present. Human beings keep roaming around in the jungle like a deer having saffron within it all around uselessly for it. It is in love the fragrance is coming out of his own belly button. The same way a human being keeps running around for happiness and pleasures whereas all the source of happiness is within him in his soul.

The meaning of happiness is not always in self welfare or the fulfilment of your own vested interest. A selfish man always considers humans of his personal life as a parameter of his happiness. In fact happiness and progress is dependent upon the welfare and interest of all. As long as we are not able to develop the emotions of serving others with charity we are not really be able to find happiness.

Change in life does not come out only following the process of worship whereas it can be possible by changing the thinking and finding the knowledge within. The relationship of happiness is not where it is related to various journeys towards religious places, instead it is a state of positive mentality.

Human beings have been taught for centuries that it is not just a body basically is a soul. The man of the century has come to know literally and intellectually that all the living beings of this one get perished only through their outer body, there soul never perishes. Why doesn't it parish? The deep secret of this is usually apprehend able. What we mean by soul that is through our own thought process and also from the experiences out of our deep thinking on death and life. These experiences are not easily expressed in human beings' life. Whatever thoughts, experiences, emotions and liking he observes in his life at most and with which he is more attached knowingly or unknowingly all that will become a part of his own self analysis. If a man gets eligible when life is forgetting himself is trouble from within along with being strong then after this birth is meeting with the Almighty maybe possible. In fact life is beautiful, positive and hopeful but one thought always freaking human beings which is called death. To get out of this life cycle and state of birth continuously there is one best possible way out- get yourself totally imbibed in the Almighty.

This is the only all-time way to get rid of the cycle of birth and death and the desires and hatred during the life. This is what considered appropriate for a human being. But to follow this path is not easy. In order to devote himself in God, a person has to indulge his life in the sacrifice and philanthropy for the happiness of others. Following this will boost our inner-self. Getting assimilated to the inner-self within means get rid of tension, meanness, deep desires about life and the things around and it is in the direction to develop our inner-self for the concentration in the efforts towards reaching to God.

Undoubtedly this deed will not make our body imperishable and perpetual but it will lead to us towards the Almighty deviating ourselves from web of death and life. In fact only God is the source of the conduction of life for all the beings in the universe. Since this source of conduction and God Himself is not attached to the cycle of life and death, this is why we also should try to be a part of that process.

A human being starts getting the element of self-knowledge through the constant efforts. His real change starts only after he starts towards the path of self knowledge. The ultimate power is not attainable through senses still with help of consciousness it is sensible. The Almighty being beyond the reach is the challenge for us that we recognise the limitations of our wisdom. After this we should proceed further in the direction of self knowledge under the skillful guidance. Proceeding in the same direction only brings the state of self-realization. The Buddhism of Buddha is the realization of this element only which should be called the dimension of divine knowledge.

Understand what the saints say

Our saints have been goading us towards right path from the time immemorial through their great life, sacrifice and noble deeds. Without caring for life the saints develop such a faith within which one has a boundless creativity with trust. They do not get stuck in the physical and intellectual knowledge, but keep trying to behold the Almighty in the relative consciousness. In fact the physical knowledge is incomplete and broken whereas the self knowledge is intact, self-proven and perfect. After reaching to the stage of such knowledge the senses of self-realization appear. The stage of self-realization is itself visible just like light.

So often what the saints or noble people say, have a deep meaning within. A man should always be in good company paying attention to the real meaning of such words. Unfortunately we are not able to understand these things. This would be wrong in case of any person that he could not get a good company and good opportunities in the life ever. In fact we get good company of good people and good opportunities too but not able to get hold of them due to being in influence of our body and senses.

The words of the saints is so often sound difficult to comprehend. Only a person who is pursuer of Yoga and good path can understand the words rightly. The life of a saint is full of nobility. This nobility itself is the symbol of speciality. We should absorb such things in life.

We are very lucky to have a company of the people with quality. This is a blunder if we lose this opportunity. Such opportunities do not come back every so often. We need to have memory and ability to understand and remember such opportunities. We should always remember that we also have a good soul within us. We are not able to keep it within our unclean behaviour. This is possible through the help of good company and the practice of Yoga. This is a perpetual truth that everyone in the world has the element of God in him or herself. As much as is this element within me the same way it is in everyone in the society.

All souls are basically the pure place of God. Everyone should keep looking for the God within himself. Doing this a person is able to eliminate so many bad qualities automatically. When an individual starts having satisfaction within self through Yoga and Satsang, then he does not need anything else. He himself gets to realize the spiritual elevation in any state. There is in fact no bigger religion than Satsang, good deeds and satisfaction. A dissatisfied person does not get satisfied no matter how much he is being given. He thinks it is injustice being done to him.

On the other hand a person who is satisfied with whatever he gets out of his labour, happily accepts that as the gift of God.

The sense of satisfaction within is a must. This is very much required that we should utilize our money and assets of property not only for ourselves but also for the society's sake. Everyone must be benefited out of our resources. We should always try to return whatever we have earned from the society. Old sayings too have the same theme. The word like 'Daridra Narayan' is a symbol of Indian culture, civilization and human values. In other cultures of the world service has been a significant element as missionary and other charitable works. In principle, we can say that through the service and charity only we can bring harmony and happiness in the society.

We keep enjoying the pleasures of this world in our life. We also consume such things which were not created by us. We do not even say thanks to the nature by doing so. We do not say thanks to those Karmyogis also whose fruits of technological inventions or products we are enjoying today. Everyone morally feels bound to say thanks for any service or product created by others for them today. Whatever we get from the society we should return that also. The best life is when we lived for others and do the best work done for others. This is good deed and in fact this is the real spiritualism also. No religion or spiritualism can ever be bigger than a human being. This is why whatever we have we should utilize that for others also. A human's service is actually God's service.

We have to pay attention for our individual inner progress and inner developments on four points – hard work, self study, control and service for others. All these four are truly required for the elevation of our self. All these four elements are a must for self elevation. Without even one out of them we can't get the elevation in our life. All the four are complementary to each other. Upasna (worship for God) and Sadhna (constant worship of God) together give progress to our soul. Upasna means the trust in God and an endeavour to reach to Him. Getting close to God requires an endeavour from a person with all his heart, body and money. Getting close to God means realizing His noble qualities and specialities within us to some extent. The way sitting close to fire we start realising warmth, same way getting close to God itself brings goodness and good qualities within us gradually. Satsang (a company of good people) brings the same benefit.

Life will change through good company

Satsangati (remaining in good company) is a big quality of life. Even if we are void of all merit, quality, eligibility or sight, still through just Satsangati we can achieve all the four. Sitting by the side of God and getting meditated towards Him itself starts changing life itself. The plants close to the sandal tree automatically get fragrant. The real truth is only this proximity and closeness. Meaning of Upasna is this only that we keep worshiping nature and God. Each moment we should keep worshipping nature thanking it for everything it has given us. By doing this we keep chanting, keep worshipping and keep meditating. While doing this we should also realize within the noble qualities of nature gradually. By doing so we gradually assimilate ourselves in the nature and God and then in the same proportion we will also be able to getting into nature and God slowly. This process of unification gradually a human being is guided towards good path as an element of God.

Sadhna and Satsangati is very essential for life. If we do not have an ability to keep memories, our worship will not be completed, no matter what our way of worshipping is. When we get justified with our behaviour and thinking then our acceptable way of worshipping paves way for our welfare. Way of worshipping should follow the path of truth. It should be free from falsehood and pomp shows. We can make our lives rational and refined. Each moment we should keep an eye on our behaviour, quality, and deeds. We should keep checking if there is any fault is entering in our behaviour. If this is happening then we should be conscious in this direction.

One should keep the truth in his eye always be neutral in all the circumstances. Defining Nishkam Karmyog in Geeta, Lord Krishna has said that human beings should be neutral towards the result of their deeds instead they should be attentive towards their duty without worrying about the outcome good or bad. Nishkam Karmyog is the best way. Samatvam Yog Uchchyate– this emotion of samatv is called yoga. Inequality-less state of being is called Samatvam. Riddhi and Siddhi make a person in-equal, even if there is no attachment in action still there should be dedication in work. Leaving attachment in everything heard or seen without thinking of achievements or unachieved state, one should be devoted to action following the path of yoga. We should not let our heart wander and confused.

Yoga is a state of moral, spiritual and mental climax. This process proceeds slowly through hard work with consistency. In the beginning we should keep our eye on our target only. This is why trusting yoga we should follow the path of Karma (action). State of Samatva (equality) is being neutral between achievement and non-achievement. This cannot be deviated from achievement and non-achievements. It does not give birth to inequality. This is called Samatva Yoga due to this. It makes a person leave his desires this is why it is called Nishkam Karmyoga. Having the inspiration towards action it is called Karmyog. This Karmyog takes a human being towards God. This is why its name is Yoga or Mel (meeting) also. Its base is intellectual. This has to be kept in sight that while in action one has to remain neutral about the success or failure and the heart should be free from any desire. The longing towards the result fails the state of Nishkam (without a wish) Karmyog. This is why Nishkam Karmyog is also called Buddhiyog (yog of wisdom).

Each hard situation and struggle are lesson-giving to a human being. We should study and follow them neutrally. A man should keep learning even in adverse situations. If we study life stories of great men of the world we would find that pain more than pleasure and poverty more than richness has educated them. Instead of admiration, beings hurt by criticism had ignited the fire of learning within them. All sorts of knowledge be it physical, metaphysical, worldly or spiritual– all is within us only. We are full of all kinds of knowledge but we are unaware of it because our Karmdosh (errors in deeds) put curtain on them. The moment this curtain gets removed we witness to the knowledge.

After constant endeavour and practice when this curtain starts moving away we say – we are realising knowledge. All our doubts are getting clear and our vision towards the truth is getting better. The faster is the speed of the curtain getting removed the better our vision gets with the truth. The person who succeeds getting this curtain removed is known as. Omniscient. Indian history and Sanatan culture has been witnessing such knowledgeable personalities time and again.

In every age, there have been arrival of such noble souls, thinkers and knowledgeable persons. Even today, there must be so many people like them. And the times to come again so many people will keep taking birth. The way a lightening stone has fire within it the same way there is knowledge within every individual. Through outer action such as friction we get fire coming out of the stone, same way we can get the fire ignited from within. If we realize with a stable heart and analyse ourselves then we come to know that all our activities such as laughing- weeping, pain-pleasure, grief-happiness, etc are only limited till our outer behaviour only. This is our original nature but the tendencies are not original. Due to being a curtain on our soul, we are uselessly busy with these behavioural processes. Our present personality and character is the result of this only. These are all known as Karma including Ghaat (attack) and Pratighaat (attack in revenge).

We should also keep in mind that the purpose of human life is not only physical pleasure and happiness, but also the search of truth and knowledge. Pleasure and happiness has to end one day. Living in the world considering this that pleasure and happiness are the only reality, is not right. The source of all pains is this only. Human beings unknowingly consider that the consumer products can only bring happiness of life to them. After sometimes they realize where they are heading to is not pleasure but it is knowledge. Happiness and sorrow both are great teachers. The experience a person gets from happiness, he gets the same amount of experience from sorrow also.

Living in this world staying in action is our behaviour. There are many experiences we get in the field of action. This also influences us. We should have a sharp memory so that it can guide us. Pain and pleasure have their effect on our soul. They also engrave many kinds of pictures on our heart. The summary of these pictures or cultures is called as the character of a human being. If we behold the character of a human being then we will realize that it is in fact the result of his mental tendencies and mental bents. We also see here that the making of his character has been the result of his pains and pleasure equally. Human character is also a result of his social coordination and experiences. This is also the reason that good company has always been significant. Through this we are able to save us from the bad results and bitter experiences of social life.

Time is priceless

It is the meaning of a human being itself that he keeps thinking and pondering about all the works, circumstances and atmospheres. Actually thinking and pondering is the real exercise of our mind. Positive advices and excellent thinking gives right direction to our life. We should always notice what are the things about which we keep thinking all day. Time is too precious and is getting spent by each passing by moment. It can never come back in any circumstances. It is important that we should utilize time in good deeds. This is only possible when we keep on doing self-analysis and self-valuation each moment. All the tendencies, thoughts and emotions we pass by, we have to keep in sight. We have to examine our mind being a silent witness to it.

We should always keep on making efforts towards making our vision grand and welfare-oriented. We should keep ahead in the direction of making our thoughts noble. We should keep enlightening our soul by noble thoughts and good deeds. Good thoughts do not let negativity like jealousy, hatred, revenge, etc. arise. To keep our mind disease-proof we have to keep enlightening the God element within us. Each molecule within our mind is the God's particle only. We should not bring obstacle on God's path which is full of light and constructive works. If we do not concentrate strictly during study, pondering or Sadhna we will not get the expected results. Inauspicious thinking is a symbol of mental-debility. This eliminates the mental powers and enthusiasm as well. This also deteriorates the mental constructiveness and optimism. Inauspicious thinking certainly gets our behaviour dirty and deviated.

We should always do good auspicious deeds in our life time. We should always emphasise upon self and inner cleanliness each moment. All the negative thoughts like ailments, sorrow, sadness and disappointments are obstacles in the path of mental peace and progress. We should keep making efforts towards getting rid of them. A man can work excellently after getting rid of his mental negativity. The first mental ailment is his kinetic state of spiritual mind. This is but natural that mind is kinetic and our organs are moving. For controlling them we need control, discipline and spiritual power. The control over mind only can be a basis for his victories in all directions. We should goad our mind towards achieving spiritual and moral energy by making it disciplined and attentive.

Our behaviour should be justified and as per the religion. Here we do not mean religion by the process of worshipping. This signifies the realisation of duty towards the positive responsibilities towards the society and humanity. Following the path of religion this way human beings get money and happiness and also get their desired things and accurate place. Religion oriented behaviour helps a human being achieve Moksh ultimately. The Saadhak (the worshipper) has to face some obstacles initially while walking on the path of religion. The thing which keeps a person stuck into the things to do, is religion. For the welfare of the beings, religion has come into being. The person who regularly wish good for others is the only person who know what religion is. Dharmatma (the doer of religion) is that person only whose soul is sinless and character is clean. The person whose inner-self is dirty he does not have power to behave as per the instructions of religion.

There are many opinions about the power of the Almighty. There have been many kinds of opinion about the existence of God. Many opinions to see God in different forms. Some see Him in the form of nature and some see Him in the form of Sun, Moon, river and forest. Some consider Him as a human avtar and some consider Him as Guru or Paigambar. There are many people who do not believe in the existence of God. There are many people who think God has never appeared in human form ever. They say, God never has said that He is God, He is the creator of this universe. He has been there from the beginning because He has created the universe. Since when is He there, is something we cannot say anything confirmed. He himself has not been seen by anyone, still His existence is question-less.

There has been an ambience of curiosity and keenness about the existence of God from the time immemorial. Though it is said that God is present in each and every molecule of this world, it shows the existence of God, still there is no confirmed place of His abode anywhere. He is name-less also. He is addressed with many names. He has not been seen giving someone something, but He is known to be Daataa (donor). Sometimes some knowledgeable people also say that it is not God who has created humans but it it humans who have created God. God's concept has always been there for lakhs and lakhs years in some or the other form. If we consider nature as God, then God's greatness has to be appreciated. It has created humans as its best creativity. This is unfortunate that humans have not learnt anything out of His greatness.

Some of the knowledgeable people think that if there is God then the world would be sinless, crime less. If He is in every particle of this creation then there must be some evidence of His being somewhere. Some of them think that in fact God has not created humans but humans have created God as a wonderful discovery, because God being one is not displaying Himself but a human being staying just one out of trillions of people, tries to show himself off. The most loved thing for Him is His name which He loves to hear, read and watch all the time. He is always prepared to do anything for his admiration. In a general human life everyone wants his son to be like him and proceed further in the direction of his desired goals. Certainly the Almighty might have also thought so while creating humans. This is why humans should give right direction and structure to the society by following the expected and proper way of behaviour.

In fact God is the ultimate power which is present in our soul. Through it only we come to know about each auspicious and in-auspicious thing. Our all the knowledge is based on self-realization which we call estimations. The knowledge which we proceed with a common to special one has its foundation as our own realization. The science which we called a definite science, is easily understood by us as truth. We can certainly say that we can read future through them as Mathematics, Astrology, etc.

Scientists and learned people keep examining everything. They never ask us to just trust anything. They themselves have experienced subjects and reached to the principles. Every certain science has a proper ground with it and the principles it shows, anyone can understand its truth. Same way, there is a base ground for the religion oriented behaviour. Religion is not only based on previous experiences but a person without being enriched with them cannot be a true religious. The skill which makes us achieve these experiences is called yoga and Saadhna. As long as someone realizes the truth of religion, cannot understand the real face of it. When a man holds truth within him, has witnessed truth and realizes the truth in his heart then only he could get his confusions and doubts cleared.

Winning heart is winning the world

We should control our heart and other organs of desires strictly. If something wrong is being happened through heart, words and body then stopping that right away is religion. Humans do have to face the results of their bad deeds. A person's accumulated deeds do show their results later. The results of the deeds would be good or bad, depends upon the quality of the deeds. Sometimes their results show up right away but sometimes they take many births. If not today or tomorrow or otherwise in the next birth – we are bound to face the music of our good or bad deeds. Only the good deeds can assure humans' real welfare when they are determined for the moral welfare of the society and humanity. The same way the things which are considered bad on moral grounds, a person has to face its bad result some way or the other, some day or the other.

Actually all the auspicious and welfare-oriented deeds are our good deeds. Contrary to this the bad deeds in accordance with the society and civilization are symbolic to sin. We should always be involved in auspicious deeds. This way we will by itself stay away from inauspiciousness. Our deeds can be auspicious only when we come out of the polluted and narrow mentality which considers selfish and physical pleasures as the ultimate goal of life. We have to come out of this mentality. We have to think that the human consciousness is not limited to carnal body of humans. He is a conscious soul. The nourisher of the human body is the soul itself. The moment soul gets out of the body, the body starts getting ugly.

The consciousness and memories of a human being is not dependant on its body only. Its level and base is wide and holistic. Wisdom, actions, consumption, ego, greed, etc are the religion of body and mind, not of the soul. This confusion arrives due to the want of Aatmgyaan (knowledge of self) which makes an individual think that he is a body, not a soul. This body is made of five elements viz. earth, fire, air, water and sky. This is the reason the body is perishable. After death the body dies and we leave for the another destination of our perpetual journey. This is just like wearing new clothes leaving the previous one. This body is just our clothes which is made of physical elements. We are not just a home, but we are the owner of this home. We are not body, we are soul which is full of consciousness. The soul neither has any caste nor any gender. It is bound to the four Ashramas (age-wise living phases) viz. Brahmcharya (celibate phase), Grahasth (family phase), Vanaprastha (forest phase) and Sanyasa (eremite phase). Soul is neither a doer nor a consumer. It is away from all this. Away from all this soul is a watcher, an incorporeal and a gazer only.

Saadhna and Satsangati paves the way for Bodhi (ultimate knowledge). The way a candle removes darkness, same way the light of self-knowledge removes the darkness of ignorance. All the confusions also get removed with the achievement of self-knowledge. Soul is free. It is omniscient. It is not bound to anything either. Body is limited but soul has no limitation or bound to body. All the difference is corporal. Soul has no form. It is formless. That formless structure is this universe. The forms get made and gets changed but the main element within it, which is soul, remains the same. The way jewellery is made of gold which keeps changing its designs but the element of gold remains unchanged. Soul, God and Brahma (the creator of the universe) is the synonymous to each other. Our body is perishable which ultimately has to be perished. What is imperishable is our soul and yes, it is our good deeds also.

We have to stay free from all inauspicious and narrow thoughts. We have to be attentive for this. We are a victim of misdirection. The biggest victory for a human being is to win over mind. If there is something we have to win in this world then it is our kinetic mind and longings. All the inauspicious thoughts which come inside his mind is due to our longings. All the good thoughts are due to our self. Inauspicious thoughts leave all kinds of impression on humans' personality. This not only decreases physical power but mental power of thinking also. Being indulged in in-auspicious thought, the self power of human beings also deteriorates.

To keep away from bad thoughts, one should constantly remember nature and God. Through this the self power can also be increased. Self-confidence is a must in any arena of universe. If we have self-confidence we can make even impossible possible. We every day spent lots of time on traffic jam, phone and social media, but if we spare just a little time for yoga, Sadhna and meditation, then our life can get a new and proper direction.

The corporal pleasure is momentary. The achievement of the perpetual pleasure is only possible through the soul. Living life with pleasure is an art and one does not need to look for that pleasure outside when it has to be searched inside. A man can make each moment of life happy through good behaviour. If he lives each moment valuably with memory then he can achieve the state of perpetual and constant pleasure.

Certainly if a person is not self-aware and active, the body-issues and grief become a permanent part of his life. They keep indulged in it only. They have longing for the wrong things and wrong people. We have to concentrate carefully on our behaviour. Being aware means keeping an eye on ourselves. One should be aware about his daily activities, his thoughts and deeds. We can do so only when we keep examining ourselves on self analysis and self examination. When we try to understand a topic and keep on trying so and stay constant in the process then gradually we become aware and active towards our thoughts and destinations. Then all mysteries slowly get uncovered. When we do not get aware and believer about our deeds then the grace of God and nature does not favour us. Through the knowledge only we get aware and memory as well.

By means of constant Saadhna we are able to concentrate. This concentration takes us to good path. Saadhna and Upaasna (light worshipping) take our life towards the path of righteousness. Constant Saadhna results in good thoughts and good emotions within us. This changes the entire philosophy of life. When we light a furnace then the way the heat spreads in the entire atmosphere of the room warming everyone in there, the same way even if a few members at home follow right-mindedness, then it will not only help themselves but others also at home to feel peace. It not only eliminates the negative emotions but also increases good-thinking, unity, love, discipline and harmony in the family.

Sadbuddhi (good-thinking) is an ultimate original power which brings all the changes in life. With this change, all the circumstances of a human being will also change. Sadbuddhi gives power to pave the way for self-observation, self-purification, self-progress and self-realization in life. The moment Sadbuddhi enters in a human's life he starts self-observation leaving the cry about his problems. He finds and removes the errors from within. He starts such activities which are not meant to deliver pain to him or others but would be helpful in the increase in ease and happiness.

One should keep making efforts to win over his mal-tendencies constantly. The rivals like desire, anger, greed, ego, etc. bring fall for us. We have to recognise and eliminate these foes. None of the foes is such which is invincible. All our thinkers, saints and seers win over their rivals in the forms of their organs of desires and that way have presented the inspiration for us. We should make efforts to be the same way, desires-winner. In today's age people are the slave of their organs of desire. This is what increasing desires and lust in their life. The fulfilment of these desires increases ego and the failure in doing so delivers anger and tension. Both the situations are not good for humans. Both ways his fall is certain. This is why it is necessary to win over ego and anger.

Certainly, winning over anger is possible. This is not an un-curable ailment. Through many processes of yoga and sadhna one can win over this foe. In normal life often anger takes birth due to normal reasons and it could also be eliminated through normal ways. Anger takes a man to failure and it also hurts people who are targeted by it. The angry man is not able to hold mental balance. People also go away from the angry person. People also hesitate to talk to him. Reason being such person may go angry any time and start fighting. The ties of these people get cut with the society. And this could be too fatal for their success in life.

Anger pollutes our wisdom. It invites destruction. Actually anger and ego get the expediency out or its house i.e. the mind of a person. Usually psychologists suggest many ways to control anger. There are many Sadhnayen (worships) and processes also suggested in spiritualistic texts to help people control anger. In practical life also our senior citizens and experienced people tell us the ways to control anger. No doubt, anger kills our memory. This destroys and misguide our thinking and behaviour. Due to the want of expediency and memory, people in anger commit such crime that burn them also in the fire of regret after some time. Obviously, if he would have controlled his anger he would have averted the situation and his entire life would not have been destroyed like this.

Certainly through Satsangati we can achieve spiritual upliftment. Company of quality people goad us to good path. When we want to live a spiritual life, we find spiritual people and can spend time with them. Fortunately if we get to achieve company of such people who have spiritual experience, then this company is even better. Going to these people we get to notice the spiritual values of life. The atmosphere there directly contacts us in our soul. The person who knows his soul has the power to make us get attracted to him. His magnetic power uplifts us and our attention gets oriented to our inner-self.

We should keep having an eye on our daily life constantly. We have to keep vigil at us if we are wasting our time with wrong work and wrong people. We should utilize each and every moment of our small-span life. We should also utilise our energy rightly. If we want to improve our meditation-practice we should think in what kind of company we spend our time. If we spend time with people with spiritualistic bent of mind then we would see our concentration in meditation is getting better. We also get more solidified on Yogabhyas (practice of yoga) and Sadhna. Our meditation practice also starts getting more fruitful. For choosing our company wisely we get inspired for marching forward on the path of spiritualism.

Desire-less Action (Nishkaam Karmyog)

Having faith in God is a good quality but it is pointless without Karmyog. The faith cannot be the reason to be action-less. Faith should be rational and valuable. Indians are very religious people. This quality has been transferred from generations to generations. We see God in each and every molecule of this world due to this belief only. On behalf of the same belief we personify God in the statue of stones. Due to this faith only we think of God in each good or bad phase of our life as our saviour. This is our trust in God that in any bad situation that power will sure come to save us. This mentality in fact, is associated with each faith. This faith also helps us recognise what is good and what is bad.

Usually we see that due to ignorance faith becomes a reason for the hypocrisy and impost. Many selfish elements do exploit innocent people in the name of religion. Even today's twenty first century of scientific world is full of such hypocrisy and impost. It is probably the most in India. Some people due to their own selfish motives make it superstition. They change peoples mind with heavy allurement, fake miracles, black magic and things like this. Their faith of trust is thrown in the pit hole of superstition.

For last many years many such hypocrites and imposters have hurt the faith of people in India through their selfish superstitions. This should not be re-repeated. Talk about Nirmal baba or Radhey ma or talk about Baba from Sirsa – Gurmit Ramraheem, many such hypocrites fill their home with money exploiting people's faith. They run the religion as a shop and present themselves as the agent of God. Power, money and people's support make their ego cross all borders. If the government takes action against them they start taking refuse in violence. What we have seen as the bloodshed and violence during Gurmeet Ram Raheem arrest, that will for many centuries show the line of difference between faith and superstition.

Due to superstition and hypocrisy, society's expediency and thinking-power goes down. This creates upheaval of ego, injustice, violence and anarchy. Only a society of rational vision and scientific approach can guide the entire world becoming their ideal. We have to awake the civilians about the religion and spiritualism. Religion is to unify the society not to disintegrate it. If anarchy, indiscipline and ego enters in religion, then such a religion gets ugly getting deviated from its original structure. We have to nullify interest out of our behaviour and all the disorders through the thinking. Without doing this our behaviour cannot compliment to religion.

The real progress of life is constantly getting rid of disorders. Following the path of righteousness life absorbs the feel of complacency. This can be possible by making the thinking positive. One should live a complacent spiritual life with faith in God and nature. This will eliminate deviations of mind. This keeps the person close to God and becomes full of moral values.

He gets goaded towards living an spiritualistic life through Nishkaam Karmyog (action without expectation) and Nirvikaar Bhaav (desireless-ness). Human civilization and this entire universe have always been respecting such spiritually great men and saints. All the saints from India and the world all have been living in the Nirvikaar state with complacency. Complacency is the base of peace. For reaching to this state one has to win over his desires. The real good behaviour is to require and consume which is rationally required. By doing this the possibility of complacency, peace and harmony is always there.

Actually our mind and our bodily organs are the source of all types of disorders. All the bad deeds originate in our mind only. If mind is changed then bad deeds will also not take birth. It is our mind only which makes us roam around here and there presenting right as wrong and wrong as right. This is why the person who is able to control his mind, never does any wrong. it is very necessary to have good human values like amicability, tolerance, morality, boldness, etc. developed within a human being since without this his life cannot be successful. The way seed sown shows the quality of the soil the same way a person is known by his culture, education and intellectual level of his. This is the original duty of a man to keep him simple and humble. Even after getting physical success he should be down to earth.

Constant Yog Saadhna and Satsangati (good company) is required for the peace of mind and control over corporal desires. Yog, Pranayam & Dhyan are the only ways through which we can keep negative traits like jealousy, ego and complaints controlled within us. Everyone should regularly involve himself in the process of Dhyan and Yog. This way everyone can proceed on the path of self-purification while purifying him from many errors. Meditation is the best way to make ourselves excellent and balanced. Through meditation we can convert our negative emotions into positive ones. This way we can convert our jealousy into love, frustration into confidence, disappointment into hope and ignorance into knowledge. A man should be creative. Every one in the world has been gifted with something or the other by the nature. We are not able to recognize the speciality within us due to being too busy in our corporal pleasures. Our state is like Hanuman who has immense power but due to want of memory he does not know it.

This is the duty of every man to recognise these nature-given qualities and refine them. Everyone should keep himself master at the display arts viz. music, dance, painting, sports, etc. serving is a special quality of a human being. This is the excellent way of keeping natural, simple and pure for us. Service without expectation is a great human virtue. Without this one cannot build his character. Instead of being action-less if considering what we can achieve, we should constantly think what good can be done by us and what we could provide to our country and society with our positive and constructive energy.

The way without Aasan (yog-sittings) and Vyayam (physical exercise) our human body cannot be solidified, the same way for executing mind-work some or the other mental exercise is necessary. Actually it's mind only which is the centre point of our entire personality. Life also cannot get on right path without giving right direction to mind. A person who has immense strength but if his mind is undeveloped, he cannot be considered a complete man. Nature has given usually all control of a human being under his mind. As long as mind is kinetic, a person cannot concentrate and put his mind on his Sadhna. In this entire universe the biggest victory and achievement is to win over mind and desires. Very rarely it can be achieved by someone. Many debilitated and harmful thoughts keep coming to our mind constantly. Certainly we have to clean our inner-self. Without cleaning our mind it is too difficult to clean and discipline our mind.

3

Simple Living High Thinking

If try to define Indian philosophy of life, spiritualism and perpetual culture in one line then we can say it like this – Simple life and noble thinking. In fact, in this world, only Indian culture is there which principally considers worldly achievements and money as secondary requirement. Practically also in Indian society saints, noble men, learned people are more respected than rich people. Indian society also has been getting inspired by such poor great men. We give emphasis on quality instead of the accumulation of money. Due to the impact of the western world, Indian society has also been erroneous practically. In India also people have started giving emphasis on money and selfishness instead of the good qualities. We have tried to devaluate the truth and simplicity. Truth is this that only through control and simplicity an individual can develop his qualities. No matter how rich we grow, if we are void of qualities, this money is of no use. This money will only be misused such as in anti-national and anti-social activities.

Though the thought of simple life and noble thinking sounds very easy but it's difficult to put in practice. So much of badness has come out of the ignorance about this mantra. Simplicity and goodness are inter connected. The person who has the quality of simplicity cannot be bad. And such a person stays away from the webs of life. Indian culture is an accumulation of qualities. We always give emphasis on this that humans should always be pure. They should live a controlled life.

He should shine his life with Saadhna. Actually through the hard Saadhna our soul becomes a part of God. Knowledgeable and quality people keep making efforts towards making their soul enlightened. They are constantly in touch with knowledgeable people. They get the content and leave the package. The person who does not have difference between what he talks and what he does, the same person is respected in the society. It is quality which is worshipped everywhere. This has to be noticed specially. Today human values are falling down. Worldly values are spreading everywhere. Human society is clouded with many evils from all sides.

It's a real truth that a person can develop his qualities only by keeping himself disciplined and have patience. Whatever wealth me do acquire, but it's useless if we don't have good qualities.

Our thinking decides what is going to be our behaviour. If our mentality goes self-centred and selfish, that would be bad for entire society. Today due to the self-centred thinking we are becoming too selfish and self-centred. Today's selfish culture of 'me, my and mine' has made today's person too selfish. What he earns, wants to consume all that for himself. Humans should take inspiration from nature in this regard, which in spite of being Almighty keeps returning all the resources to humans for their survival. Nobody has any control over nature. Nature is the reflection of the Almighty. It is limitless. Instead of being all this sun, moon, air, river, sea, flora – all are busy performing their duty bound to some invisible discipline. If sun and moon change their works or quit their duty, nobody has power to present alternate for the two ultimate powers.

There cannot be a better example for disciplined work than nature which is without an expectation suited for the welfare of all beings on earth. We need to come out of a bad culture.

Nature has also set up a coordination between day and night. We should come out of misconception and bad culture, and find out what exactly is the light of knowledge and Karma Yoga. For this we have to win over the enemies within us. A person is the friend and enemy of himself. We will be our own friend only when we have full control over selfishness, desire, violence, ego, sex, greediness. First of all we have to get rid of the enemy like feeling and behaviour for self, instead of going to find out a friend outside.

We have to follow the path of truth for bringing our life towards excellence. It can be achieved only through spiritual knowledge and good company. Falsehood helps a person's short term joy and happiness but in long-term, pain, repent and torture. No matter how momentary it's painful but it's result is perpetual pleasure and the extreme of happiness. Truth is like God. It is more qualitative than number wise. In fact truth is the soul of God and light is His body. A king or a leader who walks on the path of falsehood even with a huge army still feels scared and insecure.

A person who is follower of truth being even alone feels all powerful. Truth always wins. According to Mandukya Upanishad also truth wins not the falsehood. The invincible mountains of falsehood cannot make any harm the truth but just one flame of truth can burn down huge powerful fort of falsehood within a moment to the ashes. No matter how small number of friends truth has got still they are invincible. Falsehood takes birth as an old, on the other hand truth never gets old or debilitated. Truth is the synonym of God and Godliness.

The path of truth is auspicious

The path of truth is the path of religion. There is no need of any argument over it. Religion is the code of conduct for human life which inspires us to do our duty or one should dedicate himself for the society. In fact religion being an auspicious behaviour benefits all of us. Since the ancient times all the learned men and religion have been telling us to follow the moral values, establish them and behaviour also to be religion based. The religion is not a name of any process of worshipping or any narrow thought whereas it is a broad term, kind and well hearted thinking and this way it is another name of an auspicious behaviour.

Today, due to consumerist mentality, dwelling only means sensual pleasures and physical prosperity. Yes, it is so. People believe that wealth and material gains are equally the biggest achievement for them and through them they can have all kinds of happiness and peace. In reality, this money and material substances are transient as well as temporary. Anything obtained through wrongdoing is not permanent. We can't get many things with money. It is not possible to get happiness from money. Wealth can provide us a beautiful house but it can't help us to make an atmosphere of unity, love and pleasure. Money can help us making friends but it cannot make our so called friends to be honest or faithful of spiritual. Wealth can give us an air-conditioned room to sleep in, but cannot provide a sleep with peace. Money can buy tasty food but cannot buy us health. Money can help us get armed bodyguards but cannot make us win over fear and death. The bottom line is this that money and resources can be useful only when they are used for the welfare of the society and country. The money used only for carnal pleasures and personal happiness is just useless and no value.

All our behaviour should be like this that people follow it. Anything which the society does not find right cannot be acceptable. Many great men have sacrificed their lives to pave the way for the society. If they wanted they could have also lived a life full of worldly pleasures and materialistic. But they gave direction & inspiration to the society instead of this perishable carnal pleasure and happiness. Many great men in India from the ancient times have been inspiring us like this. Crores of Indians consider Rama as their role model. His life itself has been symbol of moral values and principles. Being the Almighty He faced many pains and struggles till the last breath. He devoted His life for the welfare of His people without getting indulged in luxuries of His royal life.

Often people criticize Rama for abandoning Sita due to their ignorance. This is not appropriate. Through abandoning Sita, Rama wanted to display the example of how to behave when an allegation on the someone from the royal family. Rama knew that his wife was innocent, but he decided to keep Sita in a sage's ashram away from palace and power until the investigation is complete. This decision was taken jointly by them. In fact the ethical changes in society comes from mass awareness and mass movement. This movement and emotion appear when in the society a great man taking middle path and from his exemplary behaviour provides inspiration and education to the entire society and civilization. Rama's recognition was also as a great leader to establish moral values, not just as king of a kingdom. We also have the great spiritual glory and philanthropy with seers like Buddha and Mahavira. The basis of their knowledge is due to their teachings. It is clear that society ultimately receives inspiration due to moral values and spiritual power.

Materialistic achievements affect individual life a little, but for the whole society, these achievements have no special value. Virtues like spirituality, popularity, sacrifice and knowledge only become a symbol of inspiration for the society. The life of the devotees teaches us that by achieving these virtues any one can become exemplary for the society. Such exemplary personalities with their creativity this creation and society is constantly moving on. Such a great men's thinking, hearing and sensation arise only from their spiritual well being and salvation. People should get knowledge from such noblemen wherever they meet them. During the ancient Indian culture, there was a rare ritual to discover the best gurus and sages by every citizen of the civilization. There is no such search of the knowledgeable persons, is seen today. Everyone is running after just wealth and physical accumulation of materialistic objects.

But this is substantial only. We have not been born to continue consumption. West's Fascist culture has made humans slaves which is still going on indirectly. Like this, it seems that today the invention of products has not happened for human, but a humans themselves have become a tool to buy these products. In such a homogeneous society, characterless, selfishness, violence, chaos are promoting terrorism and immoral crimes. These elements are misguiding the society, and it is moving towards the wrong path.

A society that is becoming morally bankrupt

Such crimes are regular in society which put a question mark on our society being capable of being called 'cultured', a word that is usually associated with modern societies. Recently, we have seen a spate of such crimes that can leave any normal person in a disturbed state of mind. Some 'monsters' crossed the limits of depravity in Cyber city, Gurugram. Not only did they commit rape on a helpless woman, but when she called out for help they threw her daughter on the ground and the poor girl died. This incident shows us how far humans can show 'mean' behavior and throttle the emotion that is called humanity. It is an incident that puts all of humanity to shame. The beasts were so heartless that they threw her baby daughter to the ground and she was dead by the time she could be taken to a hospital. Taking her daughter out in the middle of the night proved very costly for the woman. Any person who has the least bit of emotion and humanity will understand that woman's pain and grief. Those of a criminal bent of mind cannot understand this pain. It is these beasts who throttle 'humanity' from time to time and at all places.

These days, governments regularly talk of women's security, and many laws have been formulated, but it has no effect on the beasts roaming around in the guise of humans. They keep on committing crimes. Governments are unable to provide any security to the women and the police are unable to control these crimes despite all their efforts. This is natural because man is a social animal and without the transmission of moral values in society such crimes are not going to stop. The working of the police also needs to be made efficient in this context.

The administration also needs to be strict and stern with regard to crimes. If the system is not strict about crimes, it will not stop. There are many categories of criminals. The first category of criminals commits crimes because of ignorance. They can be brought to the right path through moral education and skill training. This is something that should be done. The second category of criminals is of those who become criminals because of the company they are in. Their company should be changed and they should be brought into the company of good people. The third category of criminals is that of those who are criminals because of their inherent nature. They do not change their ways even after being given many chances to rectify themselves. Such people with a criminal bent of mind should be given the harshest of punishments, so that other criminals are deterred.

In India the tendency to glorify criminals is becoming stronger and stronger. The criminals often succeed in spreading anarchy in society on the basis of their political clout and power. They harass the average citizens. The administration keeps silent on any complaint received against them. In many cases it is seen that the victim had already registered a complaint against the person in apprehension, but because of the excess nature of such complaints the police fails to take any immediate action against these complaints. By the time they become alert, the criminals have already committed the crime. Many times irresponsible police officers do not even register an FIR from the victim's side. Eventually the FIR is filed at the intervention of a senior officer of the police or courts. After this one has to fight a long fight for justice. In order to make society crime free we have to initiate administrative changes, strict laws and social campaigns in an integrated manner.

Today, the biggest question facing society is why criminals are being glorified? If criminals succeed in disrespecting the best and qualified people of society by getting hold of such might and power, then it is proof of that society's downfall. If we want to stop our system and our society from going further on this path, we will have to rid our criminals of this sheen of power. For that the society will have to unite itself against these criminals. If the criminals and bad people can form gangs despite being a minority, how can normal and talented citizens surrender before these people despite their own vast numbers?

Good qualities are rare to find

'Maanusyesati durlabha purusata,
Punsatve punarviprata vipratve bahuvidyataani gunta,
vidyaav torthgyantaa.
Arthagyasya vichitra vaakyapatutaa,
tatraapi lokagyansya samasta shaashtraviduso, dharmematirdurlabha.'

Meaning- "It is difficult to find a 'man' amongst human beings. Here 'man' means such a person who is stable, determined, patient, brave and sincere. Even if one finds such a person, it is extremely difficult to find "vipr" in them. Here 'vipr' means a person who is endowed with such positive qualities such as generosity, kindness, thrifty, softs-poken, self-controlled and totally disciplined.

Out of these also it is very difficult to find a person who is "multi-knowlegeable", meaning a person who is well versed in various fields of knowledge and arts. Whether it is science or arts, technical knowledge or environmental science, politics or society, culture or civilization or historical knowledge- such men are eligible in various fields and are storehouses of knowledge.

Amongst these people also, there are very few who know the meaning of knowledge, and whose knowledge is not limited to books and is merely theoretical. After this, even if one finds such great men, it is difficult to find those who are capable of understanding that knowledge in layman's language.

Even if one finds rare people, there will be very few who have a practical understanding of the average person. There are very few scholarly administrators who understand the emotions, feelings and ambitions of the average person and his limitations and his qualities. Among these people it is difficult to find a person who are versatile in all fields, whose every action whether it is sitting, eating, sleeping, thinking-is based on religion. Such people are rarely born on this earth time to time. It is because of their incomparable personalities and acts of welfare that society finds a new direction and vigour.

We should constantly strive to surround ourselves and be in the company of talented and capable people. The manner in which darkness is dispelled by the rays of the sun, similarly our deformities die just by being in the company of the good people. A person should definitely stay away from negative thoughts. Only a person who understands the reality of life and does his work by assuming the form of an observer can stay away from negative and impure thoughts. All types of diseases, grief, unhappiness and thoughts of disappointment create poisonous germs in the brain. That is why we should try and remain free of such emotions. If the bad thoughts in our mind are banished, it comes back to its original pure state and becomes capable of discharging all duties in the best possible manner.

It is because of our wandering and fast pace of the mind that most of mankind is troubled and disturbed. The mind is a wanderer by nature, but the tendency to flit from one flower to another like a multi-colored butterfly is wrong. What is required is to concentrate all the tendencies and overcome them. The mind will definitely waver after some time, but it can be controlled with regular practice and patience. This process takes some time. It is possible only with constant meditation and Yoga. One need not get disturbed during this process. When this process is done regularly, the mind becomes determined. The best exercise for the mind is meditation. We should do our assessment ourselves.

In the form of an observer we should constantly check where our thoughts are heading. Accordingly, we should try to control them. We should alertly keep our eyes fixed on our behavior. We should be our own biggest critics. We should be free of the feeling of hearing our praise and of sycophancy. We should think of every person as our own and try to obtain knowledge and advice from him. Every person is valuable. We should always keep in mind each person's prestige and dignity.

To consider every person as a human being and being human towards him is what actually religion is. We have to abide by this religion. This is the only good deed. This awareness and empathy of goodness is the basis of balance in nature. Thinking of the welfare of others is the basic mantra of the progress of all creation and nature. Each atom of this creation and nature is tied in this chain. Whatever we take from this creation, nature and society should be returned by us and it is our fundamental duty to do so. If trees, plants and creepers take in sunlight, water and manure, then they also give us flowers, fruits, food and scents. If rivers and lakes take water from the mountains and clouds then they also irrigate the earth and land.

Balance is required in nature. As a unit of society, each person should make the basic principle of 'Pay Back To Society' an integral part of their behavior. It is a sad fact that in this modern age we have forgotten this basic principle because of losing a grip on our mind and senses. If, today, both man and society are unbalanced and not at peace, the reason is that we do not consider society as a part of us. We do not consider the good of society as our own good. We feel that even if the entire society is not benefited, we should be benefited. It is because of this polluted mentality that we are getting deeply immersed in corruption.

There are innumerable people in society for whom corruption has become a way of life- an integral part of it. They do not pay attention to their behavior. They have made corruption a natural and normal part of their lives. They often find themselves in a moral dilemma over this. They are forever confused as to whether moral values are more important or material gains. Our society can only be free of corruption when we become free of our personal interests and think of society as our own. We will have to put an end to the selfish thoughts and the flawed thinking that has taken over our society. We will have to work with the feeling of others' interests and welfare of society.

Ancient Indian values say that taking something that is not yours amounts to stealing. Monetary gains that are obtained without work have also been kept in this category. We should carry out our duties without having any expectation from anyone. Obtaining something in return for one's deeds is contrary to this feeling. Obtaining money without doing work pollutes our character, behavior and humanity.

A person's character is formed on the basis of his thoughts and ideologies. Every society and person will have to accept that corrupt behavior and bribery are immoral acts. This education should be imparted in schools and the process of character building should begin here itself. Children should be taught that they have to work for the good of society. Citizens should themselves criticize corrupt behavior and immoral acts. Every person will have to actively work to free the society of corruption.

A person who believes in working thinks it proper to lead his life on the basis of his capability, talent and hard work. He thinks that it is below his dignity to have any expectations from anyone. If every person works and has some skill, then there will not be any pressure on one person in the family to earn more money in order to sustain their lives. If a majority of people in a family work the chances of corruption will become the least. At a personal and societal level, citizens should make a resolution that however difficult the situations may be, they will neither give bribes or take bribes. In this manner, a different group will take birth in society; one that will be different and special from those who harm society for their own selfish interests.

Our interest is inherent in the interest of society

If society and systems are proper, we have no need to accumulate excess of money. In developed countries, the system and society keeps good care of its citizens. There is no discrimination or injustice with them. When the system and society provide the citizens opportunities to move ahead in education, health and other fields the citizens naturally become free of any responsibility towards the country and society. We have to create such an environment in India also. In India, there is more corruption because in the normal course people do not get adequate opportunities for education, health and careers. The work that should be done by the system has to be done by the individuals.

Since the Indian people are gripped by uncertainty about the future, they have a tendency to accumulate money. They have the fear that if some economic problem occurs, there will be nobody who will come to their aid- be it the society, system, relatives or friends. It will only be the money and resources that will help at the time of need. That is why they do not refrain from doing unholy acts in order to accumulate ill-gotten wealth. There is a need to make fundamental changes in the administrative and social system if we have to get rid of corrupt practices in every field of life. And without establishing moral values in society, there is no possibility of any systemic change. For this, we will have to make a beginning by changing our behavior.

Today, changing and refining ourselves is the biggest task before us. We will have to ignore the time it takes and start changing ourselves. We actually see what our mind shows us. If we think well, everything will appear good and if we think wrong, everything will appear bad. The difference just lies in our way of thinking and our vision of things. When the darkness of our minds is dispelled, we will feel the reality. Change in society cannot be brought about by the efforts of a few people. For this extensive and whole-hearted efforts are needed. When each person in society is tied by bonds of mutual affection and brotherhood, only then will the injustice and inequality that is rampant in society, be eliminated. When there is no inequality in society, then it will be fit to be called an ideal society.

Moral values are established, encouraged and accepted in an ideal society. Such a society can fight crimes and wrong practices. There should be a feeling of fear and condemnation of crimes in society. For this, the governments and administration should not lag behind in taking strict measures. Various laws have been enacted from time to time in order to instill the fear of the police in criminals and to rein crimes. Punishment should not be kept pending for long periods in the case of hard core criminals and terrorists. They are kept away from punishment for long periods in the name of the judicial process. This sends a wrong message in society. The average citizen is discouraged and fearful of this process.

Criminals of proven nature and hardened terrorists should be punished as soon as possible. Recently, thought was given to bringing the 'Uttar Pradesh Control of Organized Crime Act' into use. Under this law, if the crime of a criminal is proved, he can be given a sentence of upto 3 years in jail or of being hanged to death and a monetary fine of 25 lakhs can be imposed. The only objective of the government behind this strict law is to make the State crime-free, so that the citizens can lead a secure life, especially women. As important as it is for such laws to come into existence, even more important is their correct implementation. Such types of laws should be enacted and properly implemented.

Till the time the normal population does not do good deeds without fear and with confidence, it is not possible to establish a healthy society. It is surprising that even today such policies and laws need to be made on topics that should be a normal part of our daily lives. Why do we need any government program to make our country and society healthy and clean? If we want to rid our society from filth and epidemics, why shouldn't the citizenry make an initiative? Do we depend on the government for running our houses and our daily lives?

If not, why does this fact not pertain to our society? Why can't we consider public places, roads and society to be our own?

Today, if much needed campaigns such as the 'cleanliness campaign', 'Education for all' campaign or 'To save the environment campaign' or the 'Beti bachao' campaign are not able to gather the desired momentum, one reason for it is the lack of fellow feeling at some level or the other. The effort to remove this can bring about a big change, because people are already active in taking these campaigns forward since a long time. Why don't all of us become a part of these campaigns? When this whole country is ours, then how can the work of its improvement lie on a few people's shoulders? It is not proper that we put the onus of every big task and objective on just the government and the system and ourselves remain passive and directionless. The creation of a nation and society is only possible with the good behavior and hard work of citizens. Governments can make plans, but the achievement of results depends on the behavior of citizens. If our behavior is not correct, then howsoever good the plans and laws, society will not get any good result from them.

Behavior is the key to good things, not plans

The reality is that governments cannot do everything. Merely making laws is not the answer to every problem. More important than laws and projects is the awareness of society and the integration of society on matters of national importance. Good results will only be achieved when laws are implemented in a proper manner. No doubt this will only happen when each citizen of the country feels that it is his fundamental duty to abide with the law and order. There have been many instances when the citizens of this country have shown a proper display of their responsibilities. The country invariably gets united in times of crises. But the question is why do we need crises in order to get united? If we are united even during times of peace and calm, and make all efforts for the country and society, then the country will not face any crisis.

The citizens of this country have shown their unity in the face of the various wars it has fought, in the natural calamities that strike it from time to time and recently in the wake of demonetization. The manner in which the citizens have got together and supported these decisions is an example in itself. These examples have shown that there is a feeling of resolve amongst the people. Another example like this was shown in the case of abiding by GST. If a change that so big as GST post independence could be brought into effect so easily, it means that people have started adopting a relaxed attitude towards change. After such a change in attitude the only thing that is required is to speed up this process and become a participant in it. If this can happen, then the dream of creating a new nation that is being seen, will not take a long time in coming true. The dream of India can be different for different people, but there must hardly be any person who does not want to see India make progress as an equal opportunity, mighty and prosperous country.

Today, it is the demand of time that our every act should be for the good of the country. Not only have we to behave in a proper manner, albeit we have to see that those who are in contact with us also behave accordingly. For this our own behavior has to be worth emulating. We should free ourselves of all sorts of bad thoughts and narrow prejudices and live a natural and transparent life. A person should be transparent like water and have the tendency to adapt himself according to the situations. Stagnant water soon becomes dirty. Similarly, we should not let any adverse experience remain in our minds and souls for a long period.

It is important for man that he should become patient and tolerant. He should not be late in asking for forgiveness or giving it. Forgiveness has a lot of strength in it. Not only does it purify one's soul, it also wins over the other person's heart. It has the power to destroy enemies such as violence, revenge and anarchy. It creates a situation of unity and oneness in the country. Many times it happens that it becomes very difficult to forgive a person who has given you pains and the feeling of revenge becomes very strong. If the act is not anti-social and is a result of situations, one can think of forgiving such faults. One should focus on good changes from a positive viewpoint. When one walks with others, new possibilities take birth. This takes away a person's self-centredness and he is attracted towards the feeling of "Vasudev Kutumbakam".

Self-analysis and self introspection should occupy a prominent place in our lives. We should continuously keep an eye on our feelings and behavior. All the grand texts of every religion propound that till the time our attention is focused on the faults of others, we cannot enter our own lives with any depth. We cannot hide our faults by criticizing others. We should keep on looking at our faults for our betterment and change. Without this we cannot live life in its totality. This is the situation when we can get victory over our compulsions and weaknesses. The reason for this is that normally a person feels that his faults are small while the faults of others are big.

In the context of seeing our faults, the direction of politics and religion is totally different. In politics, a person who is seen to be capable of seeing the faults of others and interpreting them is thought to be a great scholar. It is expected from a skilled practitioner that he should get rid of all faults that come in the way of purification of his soul. The welfare of a person and society lies in doing away with one's faults.

Healthy Meditation, healthy body and mind

In order to overcome tensions and suffering in our life we will have to develop a positive outlook. Often we find that the situation inside and outside our home is not of a harmonious or helpful nature. In such situations, we become tense. If our mind becomes tense, how can our body remain healthy? Many physical problems and diseases also give rise to tensions. If we keep our mind healthy, our bodies will also remain healthy. If we leave behind all tensions, we will be able to discharge our duties happily. If we remain immersed in tension, our age will also be affected. That is why we need to free ourselves of all tension.

It is important that we make a habit of living without tension and adapt it as a way of life. For this it is also important that we meditate daily and take advantage of the company of good people and saints. Not only should we regularly gain knowledge from the enlightened souls, but also make that knowledge an integral part of our lives.

Man is known as the most intelligent living being who also has the best memory. It is surprising that man's behavior is becoming selfish and directionless. Man is not able to make use of his nature given intelligence and memory power. Selfishness, greed, violence and arrogance have become ways of life. Because of these faulty tendencies, there is a fast decline of the traditions, moral values and decent behavior in our homes and society. Crimes inside our homes are on the rise and a question mark is being raised even on the behavior of our close relatives.

Moral values in society are falling. Crimes take place because of selfishness and greed. Every day news is published about crimes that take place that have no sense to them. Recently, a juvenile boy in Allahabad shot his father who worked in the police department just because his father constantly used to tell him to study. Not only this, many incidents take place where because of normal advice of the parents, children become so disturbed that they have absolutely no hesitation in killing their parents.

Actually, what every parent wants is that their future generation should make more progress than them. They make their children aware of the pitfalls by citing examples and instances from their lives. This should not be taken negatively. The objective of their little interference is this only; there is no motive of their own behind this. It is surprising that these children do not understand the feelings of their parents and destroy their own future in a matter of minutes. Children are often not able to control themselves because of a negative approach and the mentality of wanting to be self-independent. There is a lack of socialization and values in them since they are used to live in nuclear families from a young age. Today, the only companion of the new generation is the mobile phone and the Internet. One wonders what sort of a country will be created by such children and by the future generation that has been brought up in this environment.

4

Money not required, values are required

It is certain that the new generation has not obtained any knowledge regarding moral values and principles. Because of the growing trend of nuclear families, the knowledge that the new generation is getting is limited. Since they are not getting the good company of the elders of the family, they are being deprived of the essential qualities and knowledge. We need to change the situation. Parents will have to take the responsibility to see that their children should get all the basic education. They should understand that they are not just fulfilling familial responsibilities, but also understand that their behavior, educational level and other qualities are reflected on the process of making of the society and the country. It is necessary that society accept that every child is an asset of the country and the proper upbringing and character formation of the child is also the responsibility of the entire society and nation. When all these work together, then only will the actual process of society formation speed up.

Our lives should be natural and simple. When we are natural and balanced, our mind does not waver. A concentrated mind is the key to all types of good qualities and knowledge. There is no doubt that naturalness is the basis of nature's administration and all working systems. A normal behavior makes life meaningful.

A natural feeling is nurtured and fed by purity, truth and Godliness. When there is no possibility of doubt and suspicion in our feelings, there will be nothing to hide. This will automatically show transparency in our work. Donning a cover, or wearing masks and twisting facts are done for selfish gains.

Our life should be natural and simple. Your natural aspect develops honesty, simplicity and fairness in your attitude.

The primary condition for a person's holistic development is that he should keep himself away from artificiality and hypocrisy of behavior, interaction and speech. When his behavior and speech are not natural, many types of misconceptions and bitterness take birth. Normally the feelings of jealousy and envy are not found among people who behave with self-confidence and who have backing of moral values. It is very difficult for a person to keep his behavior and speech natural and balanced. It requires regular practice, meditation and self-analysis.

We need to make ourselves educated, trained and skilled in our social lives. If a seed has to become a tree it has to be nurtured with a fertile soil, rainfall, sunshine, wind, etc. Similarly giving a form to dreams, objectives and successes needs a proper environment, conservation, enthusiasm, hard work and good education, etc. It is necessary to have a positive attitude in order to achieve dreams, objectives and resolutions. For this, creative and positive energy is required in life. We cannot do our best work under stressful conditions. It is important for the mind to be happy and full of self-confidence.

We should try to gain a victory over all our doubts, fears and worries. Remaining in doubt leaves a bad effect on our health. It creates a feeling of doubt and disappointment in our mind and we are unsuccessful in fulfilling our dreams and resolutions. When we are able to make our daily life happy, our outlook about our dreams and life also becomes very clear and creative.

An optimist naturally gets the self- confidence and enthusiasm to move forward in all spheres of life. It has been proved by many experiences that often people who are successful in life are not possessed of a unique intelligence. They are also ordinary people like us, but they have the ability of doing things differently from us, and thinking in a creative manner, and have positive attitude.

We are our own biggest enemies

In order to make our behavior pious and beneficial we will have to enlighten our souls with spiritual knowledge. It helps us in attaining enlightenment. A knowledgeable person is free from all sorts of doubts. He attains victory over all the enemies that are present in his being- lust, anger, greed, attachment and arrogance. This is necessary. A man is his own best friend and enemy. When a person is able to conquer his senses, he becomes his own friend. The person who achieves victory over his self, is the one who can be free from anger, lust and arrogance. In the Gita, Yogis Shree Krishna says that anger gives rise to doubt, and doubt disturbs the mind or intellect. When the brain is disturbed, logic gets destroyed. When logic is destroyed, the downfall of the person begins. Anger is an emotion and it takes almost every person in its grip.

When our anger is not under our control, it becomes destructive. Anger affects our life very adversely. It is necessary not to let anger go beyond a certain limit. Many psychologists believe that the healthiest manner to show one's anger is to express it with determination but without getting aggressive. This actually means that one should be balanced in one's behavior. We might not be able to get rid of reasons that give rise to anger, but we can surely control our aggressive tendencies.

Mahatma Buddha has propounded very logically in the context of anger. He says that in a situation of anger a person mostly does harm to himself. He says that such people are strange who show anger at the mistakes of others. Strange because, the mistake is being made by someone else and the people are punishing themselves. If I abuse you or say nasty things to you will get angry. You burn in anger and turn to ashes. The other person is not affected. In this manner, we continue to hurt ourselves. Our attention is not drawn to such a logical thing because of our anger. A person who is angry cannot think of anything else and he loses his temper and senses.

In the Shastras, anger has been compared to fire. It is the nature of fire to burn things- similarly anger burns down a person. Anger is the reason for all types of violence, disturbances and anarchy. Mahatma Buddha says that those people who give up lust, anger and jealousy are the ones who have the right to attain 'Nirvana'. According to modern psychologists, it is possible to have control over anger. Today, many types of techniques and practices are being used for this. These days many types of clinics and specialists are there for ridding people of tension and anger. Today, people have begun accepting the fact because of their anger that they have had to undergo a lot of destruction and loss in their personal as well as professional lives. It also creates a lot of health problems.

A person's feelings and thoughts should be pure and healthy. This gives you a lot of good results. Ultimately, thoughts will be formed according to one's emotions and thoughts from your perspective. A clean and pure feeling lights up the path of development in a person's life, whereas negative feelings create obstacles in the path. If we think good of others, do good deeds unto them, they will also think good and have good heart. According to science, there is a reaction to every action. When our act is good, we will get good results from it. We should also not worry about the fact that there is no guarantee that doing good for a person might not result in the other person also doing us a good turn.

In such instances, the feeling that should be there in our minds is that we did what was possible and now we should forget about it. It is better to leave the other person to do what he wants.

It is arrogance that gives rise to anger. Arrogant behavior is the reason for the downfall of human beings. When we are in the grip of arrogance and selfishness, we do not find any solace in good advice or good thinking. We start liking sycophants and liars. Our ancient philosophers have rightly said that when a ruler, king or ordinary person does not let a qualified advisor to come near him, he himself walks ahead on the path of his destruction. We should rid ourselves of all faults and welcome good thoughts and criticisms with a healthy mind. We should take advantage of such thoughts and do a self-analysis. We should welcome healthy criticism for our own betterment. This gives us an opportunity for some soul searching.

We should keep analyzing criticisms on the basis of good and bad qualities. Every person should carry out a test of the positive feedback that he receives. And conversely meaningless criticisms should be ignored. There is also a need to test the credibility of criticism. Many a time people criticize you out of jealousy and envy. There is no dearth of such people in the society, and we need not pay attention to such people. We have to develop the understanding and capability to absorb criticism on the basis of its credibility. We should also refrain from criticizing people. It brings no benefits. It is just a waste of time and energy. It adversely impacts our behavior and thoughts.

It is a fact that when we are looking for faults in a person, one finger points at him, but four fingers are pointing at us. These four fingers are directed at us. When you have certain faults, you have no right to find faults in others. If you want to save yourself from a terrible thing like criticism, we should instantly make a habit to find good in others and to follow those qualities. In certain cases Indian sages have said that criticism is very important for self-analysis. The person who criticizes us makes us directly aware of our faults and weaknesses, which our friend or well wishes might not be able to do. From this example one might think that criticism is a good habit, but if we look at the negative aspect we will realize that we should steer clear of it. It is good to change oneself after being criticized but we should not involve ourselves in criticizing others.

In reality the reason for all the pains what we suffer lies in our own self. Because of our small intellect and short sightedness we become our own enemies. We surround and envelop ourselves with lust, anger, greed, attachment, selfishness and arrogance and start destroying our own self. The reason for all our grief is our inferior intelligence. It is this inferior intelligence that keeps us bereft of happiness and embroils us in all types of fears, unhappiness and problems. Till the time this weak intellect functions, we are not satisfied with all the happiness at our disposal. Some problem or the other is always in front of us. No sooner has one problem disappeared that another one comes up. One needs a good and virtuous intellect to get out of this difficult situation. Without this it is not possible to achieve mental peace.

Being inspired by ignorance we search for temporary happiness and take various steps for its achievement. If we are unable to obtain them, or lose it after some time, our hearts get filled with anger, envy and unhappiness. This further increases our ignorance. This creates more feelings of 'I', 'me' and 'mine' and mental defects become stronger. In this manner we go further and further from the truth. Turning one's face away from this path and trying to reach nearer and nearer to the truth is the path of salvation. Purity and humility are necessary. We should have belief in our minds that God is present inside us, and all around us. We should follow the truth by meditating on the usefulness and viability of this life.

Today, people do not look at their own defects but search for faults in others. This type of thinking and behavior is not correct. People with such negative thinking harm themselves and society. They take pleasure in demeaning others. It is because of this weakness of character that we have stopped observing our own faults and are busy criticizing others. We waste our time in making finding faults in our neighbors, people known to us and other people in society. The result of bad mouthing is never good. If we want to make progress on the path of happiness, peace and self-confidence, we should tread the path that is one with religion. We will have to put reins on criticizing others and always keep our gaze fixed on our own faults.

What is right for human beings is that he should first look at himself and keep on analyzing himself with regard to his behavior and thoughts. Till now, we have considered being happy as the biggest achievement and desire of life. Because of sensory pleasures and materialistic desires, the establishment of moral values, logical behavior, sensible debates and philosophical thinking is quickly getting eroded. Good debates and debates in the context of establishing qualities have been almost excluded from the perimeter drawn by the modern culture. It is a debatable issue that if all of us became self-centred, then how will humanity be saved? This society will not remain an 'association; it will be reduced to a crowd of people. It will be difficult to have any sort of exchange of good ideas in this group.

Pay back to society

The circumstances in which a man wants to lead his life are not under his control; others are also responsible for them. He needs a clean environment, a nutritious diet, a dependable system of mutual rules, security, and certainty. The environment in which man is living today is the contribution of a lot many people. Each second we are taking something or the other from creation. We use and consume a variety of resources, things, products, scientific discoveries, etc. in our lifetime. All these have been developed before we were born by some great men and whose benefits we obtain during our entire lifetime.

We should think that if we have consumed lakhs of products that are present on this earth, what have we given in return? Will we remain mere benefactors? We will make no contribution towards nature and society. We should think of giving back something to this society and to nature for all the free amenities that we take from them. If nothing else, we can all make a contribution towards tree plantation, water and environment conservation and spending as little resources as possible. We will be able to leave behind a better environment and resource-rich earth for our future generations.

Our outlook should not be narrow. We should accept that our benefit lies in the benefit of society, the country and the entire creation. Without the society and the country being benefitted, we cannot expect to benefit. By restricting ourselves to our own selves, we create an obstacle in the process that is for the good of everyone. Man wants to take a lot of things; but doesn't want to give anything. It is a type of passivity. This is the reason for the multitudes of problems. We will have to understand that man is not that physical entity that he appears to be.

Man is an inner consciousness, that is making his physical form dynamic and lively. His inner consciousness is a part of an extensive consciousness, that establishes its element in all beings. This unseen relationship is the basis of everything good. Fulfilling this relationship is very important. Being happy in the happiness of others, feeling empathy with others strengthens the relationship of our inner consciousness. When one comes out of one's own obsessive self, and good feelings arise in one's mind towards others, then in an indirect way it is we who are benefited. A man's personal grief and happiness are part of the happiness and unhappiness of society's condition. In Indian philosophy, emphasis has been laid on the benefit of others along with one's benefit. It has been said in our ancient texts that there is no greater religion than the welfare of other people and there is no bigger sin than giving grief to anyone.

Men should always try and remain creative, positive and happy. It is our social and moral obligation to keep on spreading positive energy. We should keep dispensing creative ideas and happiness in society. If a person does not respect another person's thoughts and happiness, he himself cannot remain happy. Whereas each good day in a man's life spreads happiness, a bad day proves to be a day that gives us an important experience. A balance of both happiness and sadness is required to help us lead a normal and natural life. A knowledgeable person should happily spend each day in a creative manner.

It is a natural truth and natural human tendency that what we feel to be giving us unhappiness today, over a period of time it becomes a creative experience for us. Sadness and disappointments give us a lot of experiences and knowledge. We can never undermine the importance of failures. The real contribution in success lies in the failures that we have left behind. Human life is a natural balance between happiness and unhappiness, ups and downs, elation and grief. We should try and see all these moments as observers with a formless and unattached manner. Whatever life has given us is adequate. By adopting this approach, we can lay the foundation for a normal and contented life. Such normal and contented people are the ones who contribute towards making a healthy and well-organized society.

Qualities become venerable and worth emulating when there is a proper balance between our thoughts and our behavior. There should be no difference between what we say and what we do. For this we constantly need to practice hard and constantly evaluate ourselves. Just walking on a particular path is not hard work. Meditation, practice and Yoga have been the great traditions in India since ancient times. In the entire world where importance is given to consumerism and products, in Indian culture renunciation and patience have been given prime importance.

From Mahatma Buddha to Mahavir Swami, all great men have given this message that no greed or achievement is enough for life. They cannot be the ultimate truths of life. Whatever we want to achieve has been achieved by crores of people before us. If life could be completed just by material possessions and products, there would never have been so much violence, disturbance and anarchy in the world. The lives of Indian saints and those who gave up all their possessions for the benefit of others, teach us that our only objective should be the extensive welfare of society. Scores of saints voluntarily became destitutes but kept on walking steadily and faithfully on the path of hard work.

Even today human beings bow before these transformers of society. We remember their thoughts and try and give our lives the same direction. Their lives teach us how moral values are established in society and personal life and how to dedicate our lives for everyone's good, everyone's happiness. We should remember the great cultural heritage and the lives of the great men every second of our lives. If we are unable to get the right company in life, there is only one path of obtaining knowledge- to keep on studying the lives and philosophy of great men and philosophers.

A man is able to get freedom from political slavery, but he is never able to free himself from mental slavery. Man is not the slave of any external power, but of his own bad habits and misbehavior. We are able to obtain freedom from all types of external bondages, but are we ever free of our mental rootedness, laziness and bad behavior? Every person in society is a victim of his own bad habits and laziness. He very well knows that drinking leads to the destruction of physical and mental health, still he is habituate to some or the other form of addiction. He also knows that change can be brought about by hard work and by walking on the right path, but because he is a slave to his habits, he is not able to follow this direction. Every student knows that he can discipline himself through the mediums of studying and exercise and one can pass all the tests of life by following this regimen, but even while knowing everything he is under the influence of laziness and his wavering mind and harms his own interests.

All in all if we are disappointed, unhappy, are unsuccessful in life, it is only because of our behavior. It is clear that a man's real friend or enemy is his own self. Yogis and wise men become a part of God by gaining a victory over themselves and prove to enlighten the path for all of humanity and creation. Every person can behave in this great manner and give meaning to his life.

The only thing that is needed is to gain control over the wavering sense organs and flittering mind. We should ponder whether we have taken birth to be slaves; after all why do we accept this slavery? Another feeling that often comes to our mind is why should we become slaves to anyone. We also make resolutions to change and improve ourselves, but very few determined people are able to succeed in this undertaking.

We have become slaves to our sensory organs

Our nature, bad behavior, arrogance and wavering sense organs are constantly pushing us into slavery. There must hardly be anyone of us who can say this with self-confidence that we are not the victims of some or the other bad habit or behavior. We might not be the slave of any external force, but what about our own slavery of which we are constant slaves? Freedom from external bondage is still possible, but how will we free ourselves of our own bad habits and behavior? Without getting this freedom, the welfare of our soul is not possible. If we are unable to obtain freedom from the selfishness, lust, anger, greed, attachment, arrogance and ignorance of our own mind, thoughts and behavior, no material achievement or power can lead to our welfare. We have to rid ourselves of the bondage of our habits.

We should always be grateful for the incomparable powers and resources given to us by nature. Nature has provided us with this incomparable body, mind and power of speech. Out of these, the power of speech is no doubt the most incomparable one. Man has discovered many languages for communication on the strength of his mental capacity and talent. These languages and the foundation of speech are the basis of all the welfares of mankind. We should constantly make good use of this power. We have not yet comprehended how many and special qualities nature has endowed us with.

These are those qualities, which, if taken away will make our condition very pitiable. We do not pay attention to this incomparable wealth that has been bestowed upon us since we are busy running after sensory pleasures and materials. If our attention is drawn towards it, we will surely express our gratitude towards it every moment of our life. The difficult power of the clarity of speech has been achieved by a fortunate mankind through the good efforts of generations.

While on one hand a pure speech makes man's difficult life precious, on the other hand bitter words and misuse of speech are a disgrace to our personal and social life and take us on the wrong path. God has not endowed man with the power of speech just for communication of thoughts, but also to benefit those who come into contact with him, and also change his outlook towards life. It is clear that speech is a great resource that man has got. We can make the correct use of it only when we are full of knowledge and good behavior. The correct use of speech helps to spread good will and good feelings in society. With this we can make each particle of this creation ours.

As human beings we should be affectionate and have love for each creation of nature and God. Love and affection are based on brotherhood. They are distant from all types of doubts and logic. No doubt it happens in just one glance and without a great deal of thinking. Something that is done deliberately can be anything but love. Some scientists call this 'love at first sight' as attraction. No doubt attraction plays a big role in it, but not the entire. Because if this was the case then human beings would be most attracted by other human beings, or some other attractive life form, but this is not so. Without exceptions we see that when a person who loves something, that thing becomes the most attractive for him. That is why as a conclusion we can say that attraction does not lead to love, love leads to attraction. Behavior that is full of love cannot be sacrificed at the altar of narrow social beliefs. Love and affectionate relationships are mankind's fundamental right and duty. They cannot be ignored in any form.

When we consider every person as one of our own and keep a healthy outlook towards them, we naturally learn to absorb the criticisms. Criticisms are actually a normal part of life. They should be taken in a positive manner. Nobody can escape from criticism. The more well known personality, the more is the criticism. That is why we should not run away from criticism or be disheartened by it. Criticism is of two types- positive and destructive. Every person is a victim of criticism at some point in his life.

A critic should not be considered as an enemy. Rumors can also be a reason for criticism. Intelligent and meditative people analyze such situations patiently and logically. Many times what is seen with one's own eyes or heard by one's ears proves to be incorrect. There are many such examples when a person hears something and interprets it in another manner that is not right and harms his own self and society. One should not be impatient while taking any decision. Even learned judges give many dates in order to understand a case properly, so that all the relevant facts are deliberated upon patiently and properly.

A selfish outlook leads to many bad qualities in our personal and social life. A healthy society cannot be established without freeing ourselves from these qualities. Many times illogical behavior becomes permanent and gets accepted because of historical reasons. Some rules that suddenly come into existence have no logic behind them and it is difficult to find a scientific outlook towards them. We often see that as soon as a person manages to acquire some amount of money, riches, luxuries, his acceptance and respect in society goes up. Why didn't the same person while living all these years in society and doing his work honestly, get this respect and acceptance at that time? He becomes eligible and acceptable as soon as he became successful. In reality, the qualities of his, that the society suddenly accepted, were already present in him. The society had no interest in those qualities. Society has an interest not in the qualities of a person, but in his usefulness and in the fulfillment of the selfish interests, which is possible through their medium. This is why in India success has so many friends, while failure has many defects.

In reality we have to acquire the best qualities through efforts. Often we want to obtain everything without working hard for it. This is contrary to natural justice and principles of nature. Even an incapable and talentless person thinks that he has a right to respect merely because of his birth in a so-called high class family. Why this happens is because of the behavior of society. If we get respect without behaving in an apt manner and without having high ideals, then why will we walk on the path of strict discipline, practice, study, hard work and toil. If one gets all the sensory pleasures despite doing immoral acts and still gets respect, then why should be tread the difficult path of imbibing good qualities in life?

Similarly, people who are good looking automatically acquire prestige and acceptance among others. This can be seen from the perspective that Indian society does not give as much importance to its philosophers, thinkers, teachers, scientists and entrepreneurs as it gives to film actors. In the case of women, their looks are taken as the sole criteria of their eligibility. Whereas the life of a woman can become easier because of her looks, a woman who has various capabilities does not get the same respect in her family and society, if she does not satisfy the parameters of physical beauty that have been defined by society.

Competitions like Miss World and Miss Universe have become big businesses in the entire world. Events such as these are a proof of man's illogical nature. This gives credence to the belief that a person's color and his looks are more important than his qualities and talent. From time to time the English media deliberately imposes new actors and actresses on society in order to increase consumerism. English newspapers, channels, magazines and social media establish such incapable and inefficient actors and actresses in the form of ideal people who can make no intellectual or creative contribution to society.

Our enemies reside within us only

As human beings we should recognize the enemies that reside within us. When we are able to identify them, then only we will be able to take steps to eradicate them. There is no doubt that man's greatest enemy is his arrogance. It is surprising that he is not able to let go of his arrogance despite knowing this. He has opened the doors to his home for his greatest enemy. Some people are proud of their physical beauty, some of their riches, some of their knowledge, some of their designation, some of their upper caste. Some people become arrogant of their self– respect. A man is attached to all these different types of arrogance and still alleges that arrogance has surrounded him. He never tries to see within himself that it is he who has caught hold of arrogance. Till the time a man does not let go of words such as 'me' and 'mine', he remains unhappy. As soon as he recognizes these vices and lets go of them, he begins his journey on the welfare path.

It is very essential that we analyze and evaluate ourselves deeply. Many times we are arrogant about the good deeds done by us. We should avoid this feeling also. The surrender that gives rise to arrogance is not surrender at all. Surrender should bring peace to a person. When we are in the grip of arrogance how can we absorb good qualities. Opportunities of obtaining knowledge bypass us but because our soul and sight are absorbed in selfish thoughts we do not understand these opportunities and are not able to take advantage of them. Because of the lack of this sight we remain bereft of these qualities that we desire. We even destroy that core eligibility under the influence of arrogance that nature has given us and because of which we are considered the best amongst all of nature's creations.

In nature's eyes all beings are equal. Nature has endowed each living being with some or the other special ability. Nature has the same feeling for every being and has endowed them with hard to find qualities. Man should not be arrogant that he is the best amongst all species. There is not much difference between human beings and other animals because like all mammals eat, sleep, are fearful and have sex, human beings also do the same. The truth is that compared to human beings, animals and birds are more patient with regard to sex. It is not proper to say that man is the best amongst all species. He can actually be the best but for this he has to make efforts.

Man has to make regular efforts in order to become the best. Without meditation and good behavior we cannot claim the right to be called human beings. In that state we will remain mere living beings. A person who is a follower of truth is that who harbors feelings of brotherhood, friendship and good behavior with everyone. An ideal person is one who is free of all narrow thoughts. He neither accepts any unscientific or illogical matter, nor glorifies it. He is free of thoughts of caste, language, religion, riches and physical beauty and does not differentiate on their basis. It is such balanced and stable people who are capable of the best behavior and determined will. Only such people can give the right guidance and leadership to society. They back everyone in their hardships and problems and give all help when required.

In the modern age, there is an excess of substances and products. When man comes under their influence he loses sight of his main objectives and deviates from the right path. Generally it is seen that man often leads a self-centred life under his own influence. Either he does not think about looking at other people's sorrows and miseries, or he does not have the time for them. For ideal people such type of behavior is not considered pious. Many philosophers and thinkers even say that today man's behavior is even worse than that of animals. According to them calling human beings animal-like is an insult to animals because they lead a life that is guided by nature. They do not do any act that harms the system of nature. They are always useful to nature till the end of their lives. Man should learn this from animals and birds and should supplicate his life to nature and God, and live a balanced and regulated life.

Our behavior and our works should be the best. The type of work that we do will fetch us rewards accordingly. We will always reap the benefits of our work. A person is doomed to get fruits according to his actions.

"Jeha beeje solune, karma sanda khetaa."

This body is also called the field of action. The type of seed a person sows, the same fruit will he reap. If we perform bad deeds we will get bad results. Then why shouldn't we do such work that makes our life positive and fulfilling. When we have to do work, why not do the best and sacred works. If we want to know and get something, we should ask for the best. It is surprising that because of our short sightedness we ask God also for small things. Even our prayers and pleadings dedicated o God are not free from our narrow thinking. Even in our prayers we ask for riches, grandeur, success, prosperity and good of our family. If we want to ask God for something, we should ask for knowledge, benefit of others, detachment, donation etc., which can take our life on the path of ultimate welfare.

It is unfortunate that even while praying to God we don't know what to ask for. A seeker always asks for those things that are materialistic and non-eternal. If we really want to make our life meaningful, we will have to make our outlook, a follower of truth. We should never for a moment forget the truth of life and its true objective. Living life as slaves to momentary passions, is an insult to human life. We should never forget God and nature because when the time of our death is near, there will be no other alternative except repentance. Yogis and saints who forever remember nature and God make death also a joyful journey.

The root of 'Bhakti' lies in 'words'. Speech, words and language are the basis of all types of good work that takes place in creation. The entire world is made up of names and forms. There is a confluence of names and forms, whereas only name is there and form is an imagination. In reality, there is nothing in this world beside name and form. We all believe that God neither has any name, nor form, but as soon as we think about Him, we give Him a name and form. Our mind is like a peaceful reservoir and thoughts are like waves on it. Names and forms are methods by which these waves arise. Without names and forms no wave can arise. One form and oneness cannot be deliberated upon. They are beyond meditation. As soon as the thought becomes a thing, we give it a name and form. Both of them are essential. We cannot separate them. Nature has created this entire world with words. The Sanskrit word 'Brahm' has the same feeling that is the expression of other opinions in connection with 'words'. Principles that are popular in Christian opinion also endorse this opinion. That nature has created all things with words has a very deep meaning. Nature itself does not have any form; therefore it is a beautiful method in order to describe the different forms of creation. The expansion of this entire creation has been possible because of nature and God. Nature and God are the physical forms of creation. It is from here that creation begins and ends. This cycle goes on and on.

This creation is based on mutual affection, love and brotherhood. If this feeling, empathy and goodness is not there, the working of this world will be impossible. We constantly get the inspiration from nature to develop this feeling of love and goodness between living beings. Love is basically based on service. The definition of love is all encompassing. It is should not be confined to narrow definitions. From human beings to animals– every being experiences love in some form or the other. Man is the only living being who has been gifted the greatest thinking power and discretion. This is why the sphere of a human being's love is vaster and more widespread compared to others. A man's love can be for another human being or for birds and animals or for any creation of nature. Many people nurture and nourish plants and trees as if they were an integral part of their lives or like their children. This is the right feeling. We should love trees, streams, rivers, mountains, etc in the same manner that we love our relatives and loved ones. If such an outlook and love awakens in our behavior, this creation can obtain all the beauty that is there in this world. Beauty is not something external. It lies within us. We just need to awaken our conscience.

Do not run away from struggles; learn from them

We keep coming across stressful and difficult situations in life. Challenges and struggle are a part of everybody's life. No sphere of life is untouched by problems. We can never achieve anything if we do not face up to these challenges and struggles. Running away from problems is never a solution. Problems never come with a prior notice. And they cannot be forecasted also. Problems and challenges can be solved and faced only when we come face to face with them. We might try to solve problems on a hypothetical basis, but the results of our efforts only show when we face problems head on.

Those people who do not leave the field in the face of problems and face them in a determined manner, are the ones who defeat the problem. Those who get scared and run away from them will find that the problem comes after them with double the speed. No problem lasts forever. Wise people adopt the same attitude of equanimity towards both problems and happiness. They realize that both the situations are temporary. Therefore one should not be too attached towards anything. Wise men also know that moments of pain and sadness leave one with various experiences and teachings.

With their far sight, they make even pain and problems a device for pleasure. Similarly, during moments of pleasure wise men do not forget that these moments will pass soon. Wise men do not feel attached to these feelings and achievements. They are not gripped with arrogance during those moments and nor do they deviate from the true path. In this way, every person should try and emulate these wise men who keep themselves stable in both situations.

In reality, our behavior is a reflection of our spiritual and intellectual level. The path on which we tread is similar to our feelings. If our feeling is impure, our path will be destructive and if our feeling is pure, our path will be that of welfare. Nature and God like feelings that are pure and unsullied. A person's behavior reflects his feelings. A person who is imbibed with feelings is sensitive and one who is devoid of feelings is like a stone.

Every person has his own nature and style. Even while maintaining his uniqueness, a person can become an embodiment of all good qualities by making efforts. The life of many people is a proof that even though one may not be so talented by birth and descent, he has acquired all good qualities by his efforts and relentless practice. It is apparent that a person's feelings are transmitted all around him according to what they actually are.

If two people are doing the same work with different feelings, the results are also different. We can understand this by the fact that a doctor who works for the treatment of his patients with a selfless feeling and without taking a fee or at a very nominal fee is more likely to cure his patients. Opposite to this, doctors who take their profession as a mere business opportunity does not have the same effect. Feelings and purity improve the quality of a work many times. If there is no feeling, then there is no meaning to the work.

Nature and God also consider feelings as the most important thing because it is feelings that can reach God with the greatest ease. Neither can a person's body reach God, nor can one's thoughts affect God. It is only a pure and sacred feeling that can reach Nature and god without any obstacles. If we want to make our behavior supreme and pious we will have to remove the impurities from our mind.

5

Education should be value based

Education should be value based. Education that cannot inspire the citizens to walk on the right path has no meaning. The education that does not make a good citizen has no objective. Education cannot be considered as a mere device for nourishment of the body and a means of livelihood. This will be an insult to education. Education has a three-fold purpose- to make man useful for society, nation and this entire creation. Unfortunately, education today has been limited to being a mere vehicle for providing nourishment to the body and sustaining life. The most worrying thing is that instead of building good citizens and bringing about social awareness education is also being used as a tool for training people in terrorism and radicalizing them.

Many countries of the world have been engulfed in violence and terror because they have been inculcating their citizens with a directionless education and rebellious mentality. Those people and institutes who want to make education a means for spreading a narrow mentality will have to be stopped. We cannot allow such a transmission of education in India. Education that is imparted in the name of religion, and doctrines, divides the country and society. Education needs to be made progressive and advanced. Efforts have been made in this direction and they should be sustained. Unscientific and religious education that has no logic and the education that is imparted in Madrasas should be reconstituted and organized in a proper manner.

Many State governments have tried to impart a correct direction to Madrasa education. Some State governments have started helping the Madrasas financially. It is essential that State governments pay attention so that 'Madrasas' and 'Maulvis' do not become an impediment in the progress of Muslims. If efforts are made to propagate superstitions, conservatism and fanaticism through the means of education, then nothing could be more insulting and degrading for it. Students studying in Madrasas should also be made to clear the examinations of the recognized education boards. The subjects of education boards should be included in the syllabus of the Madrasas. When students of all religions, castes and communities study the same course material and same syllabus in a united manner, the foundation for a united society will be laid. This will also lead to a feeling of goodwill and assistance among different communities.

The triple aims of education is – to develop human being for the usefulness of society, nation and the whole universe. But unfortunately today education is mandatory for earning purpose and by all means to earn for food only. Moreover, the main worrisome factor is instead of developing social awareness and character building thought education it also involve teaching of staunch terrorism and separatism, that's very alarming situation.

Education should definitely be liberal, compassionate and beneficial for society and the nation. Often it has been seen that educational institutes are used for the fulfillment of selfish and narrow political agendas. The administration should pay attention to this. Indian, and especially among Madrasa education, seems to be lagging behind in imparting modern and scientific values. The opinion that those Madrasas that do not get financial assistance from the government can teach whatever they feel like, is not correct.

Similarly the administrative system will have to make provisions for those Madrasas that are running with financial assistance and provide with them with the correct guidance. The administration gives financial assistance so that those students who study there are able to make a proper contribution in the progress of the country and the society. We need to change our entire outlook with regard to Madrasa education. It should not be necessary that in Madrasas the teachers appointed for teaching science, mathematics, geography and social sciences be Muslim. These subjects can be taught by people of any religion and perhaps much better.

Today, it has also become necessary that Hindu, Christian and scholars of other communities should also be included in those local institutes that run Madrasas. If an Indian state helps any institute in a financial manner, there should be no discrimination on the basis of religion. This will only be possible when Muslim clerics themselves adopt a nationalist attitude to take forward this progressive thinking. The Muslim society of India needs to discard the feeling that their benefit does not lie in the benefit of this country and society and their good lies only in the religious and sect-based organizational unity.

Muslim scholars and clerics should try and prevent the spread of anti-Muslim feelings by Muslims themselves and stop the trend of making Muslim ghettos and live amongst other communities as well. If the Muslim society looks at the Islamic state with a proud feeling and gives acceptance to the violence perpetrated by Pakistan, Afghanistan and Bangladesh against non-Muslim citizens, then nothing can be more unfortunate than this. Such a dangerous anti national mentality needs to be destroyed. The Indian Muslim society has to step forward to stem such feelings. Those roots need to be attacked that inspire our people to act against the country.

Such facts are often highlighted that different types of undesirable activities openly take place in many Madrasas. It is possible that this happens in Madrasas of other states.

Government and financial sources are also misused in the name of Madrasas. Many times such students are registered in madrasas who never come there to study. It has just become the business of some people to pass them by making them fill certain forms and help them in cheating. Including Madrasas all types of teaching institutions need to be made free of irregularities.

Teaching institutes should be considered as sacred places. These temples of knowledge should never be allowed to develop as business places and shops. In ancient times, the running of schools was done by well-qualified and wealthy people of society for the benefit of society. Earlier the schools and colleges that were established by the wealthy class were made with the objective of the welfare of people, and for the betterment of after-life, not merely for commercial purposes. It is unfortunate that like other positive values and traditions of Indian culture, the Indian model of education that is for the benefit of the society, is also being neglected. An educational system that has been made merely for providing employment and nourishment to the body cannot propagate moral values in society.

Today, there are various syllabi that are popular at the educational level. It will be appropriate if a uniform syllabus is implemented for students in all the educational institutes. For the unity of the country and for citizens having a uniform ideology it is essential that a clear decision be taken with regard to implementing a uniform syllabus under the new education policy. Besides a uniform syllabus, attention should also be paid that education should not just be a medium of obtaining degrees and diplomas and for getting jobs. It is the demand of time that the future generations should be inculcated with moral values, skills and professional expertise so that they become self-dependent and emerge as national property. There is no doubt that policy makers will have to lay the foundation for a new India along with a new educational policy.

Why we are mute towards anti-national behavior

We have to guide and so the right path to the new generation. Today, the main reason for the increasing anarchy, violence and terrorism in India is that anti social and anti national organizations on a large scale are misusing the mental and physical energies of the new generation. Naxal-influenced areas and border states have many such anti national organizations that are brain washing the new generation of Indian youth. Pakistan supported separatists have converted Kashmiri children into stone throwers working on a daily wage. Actually the aim of the separatists is to make Kashmir on Bagdadi module instead of making it Islamic. They will neither live in such a Kashmir, nor will they keep their children here. They have their other luxurious abodes in other parts of India.

Terrorist and separatist organizations make the schools of Kashmir to burn, but the children of separatists cannot be seen in these schools. Terrorist and separatist leaders keep their children away from terrorism with great care. Their children are getting education in expensive institutes abroad. They are not giving them an education that teaches 'jehad' and 'radicalism'. The society has to recognize their heinous nature while there is still time. It is true that the Kashmiri citizen is gradually recognizing their motives. They are realizing that by supporting such selfish sects, the future of their children is being enveloped in darkness. Now, they want their children to get a proper education. The children are studying to become engineers and doctors. Many children have cleared the Civil Services Examination. They are being selected for the IITs.

The separatists are opposing the schools that are being run by the Indian army in Kashmir. They say that these schools are taking the children away from their culture and traditions. They should be asked which religion and culture they are following. Under which religious beliefs and cultural values does such despicable behavior fall that they are showing towards the land that has given them food, water and air? No human being can justify his behavior by betraying one's country and society and call it logical.

Despite all possible types of misbehavior by terrorist and separatist organizations the rush to join the army and police force in Kashmir continues unabated. The terrorists who come from Pakistan have no feelings for the residents of Kashmir. They are just misleading the people of Kashmir. We need to save our citizens from this web of deceit and false notions. Because of the fear of being unmasked the terrorists have now adopted another strategy. Now they are making the Kashmir police and the security forces their target. An official of the Kashmiri army had come for his daughter's wedding. He was unarmed. He was killed, but the crowds are increasing in the funeral processions of the people whom the terrorists are killing.

The relatives and well–wishers of DSP Ayub who was killed at the hands of the terrorists were shouting that they were 'Indians'. It is by developing this sort of feeling that violence and separatism can be rooted out in Kashmir. If this feeling takes root, then that day is not far off when there will be peace in Kashmir. The youth of Kashmir will hold books in their hands and not guns. They will join the mainstream. Terrorists and separatists are not the friends of anyone. They have no religion. It is a group of selfish, directionless and corrupt people that works at the behest of Pakistan for the fulfillment of their greed and political aspirations. If we want to unmask these anti-national elements, society will have to be shown their true faces. It is very important to propagate nationalist values and thoughts of social equality so that society does not become a plaything in the hands of these anti-national elements. For this we will have to give our education a proper direction.

We will have to make our education value-based. Education does not mean just the acquisition of technical knowledge and somehow nourishing the body. Today, the one objective of education seems to getting the maximum percentage of marks in the Board examinations, so that they get unobstructed entrance to the next class. Narrow syllabi are unable to develop young minds into good citizens. Merely getting good marks and clearing of examinations cannot be the sole objective of a good education. Morality, introduction to human values and their absorption, the heritage of the country, history, acquisition of knowledge and its use- all these things are surely found in the syllabi, but this is not enough. Education should be inclusive of subjects such as religion, spirituality, civic responsibility and sacrifice. It is these values and curriculum that can create awareness about the society and country in the citizens.

The biggest effort to bring about a change and improvement in the field of education in India after independence was the constitution of the Kothari commission. Based on the studies and recommendations of the Kothari commission that worked from 1964 to 1966, a new education policy was given form in 1968. This commission carried out serious investigations connected with various topics of the educational system and presented its recommendations and advice. The fundamental advice of this commission was improvement of the educational system and improving the quality of the curriculum with due regard to time. Although it is true that even after the recommendations of the Kothari commission there has not been much revolutionary change in the education system in India.

Even today the Indian education system and educational machinery demands various changes. After economic reforms, the Indian education system has become representative of even more inequality and class differentiation. On one hand crores of Indian children are not getting quality education, and on the other hand hundred of five-star schools are opening which have the most modern facilities. This difference in the education system is the main reason behind the social, economic and cultural differences and separatism in the country.

All the factors will have to make concerted efforts in order to make education a powerful tool for the fulfillment of national requirements. There needs to be a fundamental change in the outlook of the teachers, guardians and society as a whole in order to make Indian education better and useful for the people. Examinations will not be a burden when their objective will be to learn the interests of children and to decide the direction on that basis, not for making an account of their failures and failings. Marks are important, but they are not everything. There is not so much pressure on the children because of examinations as there is from incorrect teaching, uninteresting curricula and pressure from parents to perform well. When there is improvement in these spheres, the examination stress will automatically come down. Then it will remain only that much which one has to face at every phase of one's life. In order to pass in the examination of life, only marks are not adequate. We have to constantly analyze ourselves and try to raise our spiritual and moral levels.

We will have to extensively make our education system more useful for the society. In the context of the Indian education system, there is a opinion that our education system and educational curriculum is not able to substantiate our social and national needs and moral values. The system has not been able to bring the desired results in the practical field also. We are not able to develop skills and talent in our youth. All in all our education system is neither able to fulfill our economic needs nor is it being able to be a medium for our moral and social progress.

The importance of skill development and hard work should increase

Progress and economic development are necessary for all countries. The path of economic development, skill development and prosperity is also connected with improvement in education. Our Indian education system is not able to produce talented and skilled people that are required for the country. Indian students and research institutes are constantly lagging behind in the sphere of research and development. This is not a good situation. Compared to any other country, India has the maximum number of young students. Lack of talent in such a situation means that there should be extensive changes in the education system. It is a fact that the industry-business world has been regularly complaining that schools and colleges are not able to produce such students who can fulfill their requirements. The sort of moral values and behavior that should be visible is also partially because of some defects in the education system. Another big deficiency of the education system today is that it is only increasing the competition to pass with good marks. Although it had been realized ages ago that bookish knowledge has a limited importance, priority was not given to adopting new systems.

It is true that normal people who have studied in ordinary schools and colleges have brought fame and prestige to the country, there is also the fact that such opportunities are available to a handful of students. The present educational system is responsible for this. India is feeling the need for a new education system today. The best efforts are also being made in this direction. It is essential that such a direction should be given to the country where our education system should prove to be a creative device to fulfill the economic, social and cultural requirements of the country.

There should be an extensive meditation and debate on the new educational policy. An announcement has been made that a committee will be constituted under the leadership of the space scientist, Kasturirangan, for preparing a new education policy. The new policy is still not clear. At least now it should be ensured that the Kasturirangan committee should show alacrity in preparing the new education policy. Along with this it is necessary that it should be helpful in fulfilling the needs of the country. This work is surely difficult, but not at all impossible. We have to make our education system in accordance with modern times and our national requirements. It is a fact that the present education policy has not been able to fulfill national expectations.

The need for educational reforms in our country is being felt for many decades. This work should have been done immediately after gaining independence, but because of many reasons this was not done. The country has had to bear the loss of this. Even countries that gained independence along with us or after us and many small countries have overtaken us in the race of progress. This situation is extremely worrying. Our education has not been able to prove itself on social parameters also.

No doubt education should be popular and beneficial. Some radical outfits in the world have given a 'jihadi' form to education for some political ends and thrown the entire world into flames of violence and anarchy. These outfits are misusing these educational outfits to the hilt. One reason for Muslim militancy is the lack of scientific education. Our outlook should be scientific and logical.

Youth of all ideologies including Muslim ideology should be given education that has a scientific outlook so that they do not become victims of superstitions, hypocrisy and radicalism. It is especially important for Muslim youth because radical terrorist organizations give out many misleading arguments in order to lure them into terrorism. The curriculum that is used by the traditional Madrasas is called ‘darse nizami’. These were constructed in the Indian subcontinent in the 19th century.

Madrasas and the Islamic world will have to understand that toady the knowledge of science, technology and languages is very important. Without this the youth will not get opportunities to move ahead in life. Seeing the changes in the modern age, many Madrasas changed their curriculum to include “asari uloom” which means modern education, in which topic such as Computers and English are taught, but even then the students coming out of these Madrasas feel that they are not adequately equipped. Today, only Muslim children can be seen studying in Madrasas. This should not be so. If the level of education in Madrasas is raised and it is opened to all classes of society, it will be an appropriate step from the viewpoint of social inclusion.

Lakhs of Muslim children are getting education in Madrasas. Many of them obtain degrees also but when they start their working lives, they realize that the education imparted by Madrasas is not adequate to face the situations that occur in practical life. That is why they feel neglected and left out. Some of them try to learn English and Computers after finishing Madrasa education, but it is a waste of time to study English after studying in Madrasas. When religious and modern education is made available at one place, students will be able to save time. And they will be capable of competing with other children of society.

The most religious thing is country's welfare

No doubt religious education has its own importance but it has its limitations. In today's age only religious education is not sufficient to develop one's personality. Even if it is imparted its form should be such that it strengthens one's feelings of loyalty towards one's country and society. Going away from society and one's country and only thinking of one's religion and the benefits can be dangerous for the society and country. The biggest religion is one's country and love for one's country. A person who gives more importance to his persona religion, its system of prayer and traditions than to the society and country becomes a cause for providing encouragement, support and power to the anti-social elements and their activities.

In reality the Madrasa education needs to be made progressive and socially useful in the context of the modern age. In some states like Uttar Pradesh better efforts are being made in this direction. The Uttar Pradesh government has decided to teach from NCERT books in the Madrasas of the State. This decision is praiseworthy and contextual with the times. The future of the Muslim society can become bright and stable when their children get modern and scientific education. Then only will they be able to provide the expected contribution in the national mainstream. Under this decision, it will be important to teach Mathematics and Science to the students of Madrasas. The objective of the

Uttar Pradesh government seems to be to make the students of Madrasas more competitive. This is one such decision that will be gainful for the children of the Muslim society. One should worry about the progress of their future because in the past few decades they have been left behind in the race of modernization.

A demand was being made for the past many years to develop modern skills in the students studying in Madrasas, so that they could secure their future in the employment market. But despite this demand nothing much was done in this direction because of certain political tendencies. In India much talk happens about the political welfare of these backward and ignored sections of society, but solid steps are not taken in this direction. If any society has to be made progressive, the first step should be to make the education progressive and provide skill development to that section. If this is not done, then the various talks and claims will be nothing but false propaganda. Such narrow and dirty politics have harmed India greatly. Now, this should be totally stopped.

It should be ensured that education is properly imparted and accepted in the so-called minority section of the society. The belief of various reincarnations of Islam has been that it is necessary for all Muslims to obtain an education. Here, education does not refer to mere bookish or religious knowledge, but also worldly knowledge and being synchronous with it. A person can establish a healthy and balanced outlook about life through the medium of an education that establishes a balance with society. The young generation of the Muslim society should be thankful to every such person who is helping him to achieve knowledge by any means.

It is extremely important to appoint capable teachers so that the education in Madrasas improves. Without capable teachers, the efforts at imparting better education fail in the same manner that other welfare programs fail to be implemented properly in the absence of proper guidance. In 2015 initiative was taken in Maharashtra to improve the level of education in Madrasas.

Subjects like Mathematics, Science, English, etc. should be taught in Madrasas. In this context states should provide the necessary resources, financial assistance and capable teachers. The modernization of Madrasa is very essential. If Madrasa education is made useful for the society and nation a big positive gain can be had in the form of making progress and in the attainment of the constitutional objective of proper administration of law and order.

The main machinery of nation building lies in creating good citizens. The form that citizen building assumes depends on the personality and acts of its teachers. When teachers fail in their duties, there is a fall in educational values. If we want to create a systematic educational machinery, we will need eligible teachers. The role of teachers and schools is important in strengthening the foundation of the states and the country. When the teachers of a society are not eligible, selfless and hard working, the downfall of the society and country is imminent.

A major reason for our failure as a country and society has been the failure of our educational system. Our education could not garner the moral strength and qualities so that it could establish high ideals and moral values. We need eligible teachers who can become ideals for the country. The results of our efforts will not be immediate, but we will surely reap the benefits in the long run. Education is the basic tool in nation building and it should never be made a part of the agenda for obtaining narrow political gains.

No doubt that policies connected to education and teachers should be made contextual from time to time. Governments will come and go, but the country and society will remain forever. The center of our attention should always be the society and country. In reality proper importance has not been given to education at a policy level. Political parties and the society itself has paid very little attention to it. This situation should change. An adhoc opinion regarding education is not in the benefit of society. In order to make a well organized and disciplined society that is based on equality and nationality needs the level of education and teachers to be raised without any doubt.

A new educational policy should be developed

The overall educational system needs to be overhauled. Schemes like mid-day meal have reduced the government schools to 'dhabas'. It is a glaring example of how a good scheme can be badly implemented and how its main purpose can be defeated. According to the report of the Comptroller and Auditor General, CAG, it has been shown that the money that has been allotted to education is not properly spent by the State governments. From this, it is clear that the administrative system and state governments have adopted an attitude of indifference towards education. It is unfortunate for Indian democracy and society that even serious issues like education and health are never the main issues. There is no serious debate on these important topics either in the Parliament or the society.

It is the misfortune of the country that even after 70 years of independence, we have not been able to make non-expensive and quality education available to our children. On the contrary, education has been privatized, and primary and higher education is very far from the reach of the common man. There has been an unrestrained fee hike in the educational institutes of the country. Even the governments and judiciary seem to be helpless in front of these private schools. Since the children of capable officials and policy makers study in these schools, thus the schools feel safe and powerful. Hundreds of thousands of crores are spent in the construction of these schools. The construction of these schools is also taking place by some of the well-known industrial houses and influential decision makers. In such a situation these schools continue to make money despite cases of irregularities and criminal incidents taking place with regularity.

The lack of qualified and adequate number of teachers is also a big problem. Some decades ago a teacher was considered the most respectable person in society. The most eligible and qualified people of society wanted to enter the field of education. Today, the situation has changed. Today, the best and most talented students in the country don't want to become teachers. Along with respect, they are giving preference to the glamour and lure of money.

Because of the changing form and behavior of society, one sees a lack of teachers in schools. Since decades, there has been demand for the admission of teachers in educational institutions. According to the norms adopted for the appointment of teachers, a ratio of only one teacher to 120 students has been decided for inter classes. A second teacher will be available only if the student strength is more than this. Such an order has been given for balancing the teacher-strength. In this manner a second teacher will be available for high school classes if the students are more than 98 in number. Earlier teachers in middle schools were appointed on the basis of subjects, but now they are appointed on the basis of number of students.

The opinion of the government is that at the inter level it is necessary to have a specialist teacher, otherwise it will be difficult to maintain the level of studies. LT grade teachers have considered this order of the department as harassment, whereas others are afraid that if these parameters are enforced there will not be any teachers left at all to teach in the schools. The loss that this will entail will be borne by the students themselves. In this context the process of appointment should be made logical, proper and timely. We will have to make the efforts to see that the world of Indian education gets the best quality of teachers. We will need to adopt the most modern techniques and training systems for this.

Every year we see a stiff competition for admission to schools. Although schools have opened in large numbers, but the number of good and prestigious schools is vey less. There are just about one or two good schools in each town and city. All the parents want their children to study in these schools. Recommendations, access and money power are openly made use of in getting admission to these schools. The main problem of schools is that they have limited capacity for students, classes and place, and hence they cannot admit more students. In such a scenario the schools also have a terrible pressure to maintain their level of quality. Many times the management committee of schools come under a lot of pressure and even threats in order to gain admission. Even for getting admission in Nursery and KG classes recommendations of cabinet ministers, top bureaucrats and judges is made.

In India we see many problems and irregularities at the entry level in primary education. In this context we need to give form to a well-organized system. At present the situation regarding the entrance process is very odd and uncontrolled. Despite many laws and provisions having been made, there has been no real improvement. Getting an entry into good schools is becoming beyond the capacity of the ordinary person. Even if these schools are made to admit poor students, just for the sake of it, the environment there and the endless demands for the programs that take place from time to time makes it impossible for a normal person to afford.

For most institutes the work of imparting education remains limited to two technical works, i.e, providing admission and conducting examinations. As far as learning and teaching are concerned nobody pays attention to them. Our educational institutions appear to be indifferent to the process of gaining knowledge and developing skills. There is no place for a subject to be experienced at the practical level outside the classroom, and how an experience can help us solve some problem of daily life has no room in our education system.

In education, creativity and innovation are becoming mutually opposite things. Answering 'Multiple Choice Questions' (MCQs) in the name of examinations is what education has come down to. Now no student is made to fail. It has been ensured that no student will fail in examinations. The dread and terror that examinations aroused in the hearts and minds of students and their guardians 30 years ago is totally missing now. It is not enough to gain knowledge. One should have the capability to use it and to develop one's creativity because of it. The process of skill development and research can move forward only when the new generation receives quality education. For the creation of a capable and intellectually powerful India we will have to bring fundamental changes and a mental revolution in our education system.

In modern times education has been made a tool for gaining bookish knowledge and getting access to the next class. There is lack of social, cultural and moral values in education. This is thought to be outdated. Today's young generation does not want to deliberate upon subjects that are related to culture and advice. They do no take any interest in spiritual and moral knowledge. They often neglect advice that teaches us to walk on the moral path. They have a lack of tolerance.

Only that person can impart you values who himself is well bred and brought up with the right moral ethics. Today we have even forgotten to respect our elders. If we do not respect anybody, we will not benefit from his vast experiences. It is also the basic responsibility of education that there most be constant transmission of moral and social values in society.

The new generation is becoming extremely lonely and self-centred. It is these ill-trends that are basically responsible for the large number of suicides that are committed by the youth and students.

What will we obtain from a valueless education?

The objective of education is not merely building of one's career. It also has to work for inculcating values and ethics in human beings. Due to increase in ego, anger, anarchy, stress, violence, separatism, staunchness, the value of the education is deteriorating. It is often seen that we tolerate the bad deeds and harsh words of those people whom we love. And if our relationship with someone is not good, we do not tolerate even his good words. It is here that we need tolerance and this is what is required for the formation of an ideal character. Self-control and tolerance are very important for good deeds.

The great men who turned the direction of other's lives first made their own life worth emulating and full of good qualities. It is only because of the greatness of their personalities and good deeds that the society looks at them with respect. In Indian society there is a tendency to criticize others without giving it any thought. Indian education will have to take the responsibility that not only does it provide momentum to the process of citizen building, but also imbue the Indian citizens with good qualities, good thoughts and equanimity.

The education boards and administrative system will also have to play their roles faithfully to see that the education system in the country becomes better. The role of these institutions has already been determined and directed by the Constitution. At the All India level the work of CBSE is to determine the curriculum at the middle level and to increase the timely usefulness and quality of the school's management.

CBSE is a institute that has all rights regarding the studies and teachings and for making a study and analysis of the details of the examinations. While administering to its tasks, it will have to put in all efforts towards building of the nation and citizens. Presently, there are more than 11 thousand schools in India and abroad that fall under the purview of the CBSE. Advice should be taken from the teachers, students and principals and also the guardians about the making of new curriculum to the weight of the school bags and from taking advice. There should be a change in the National Education Policy on the basis of these recommendations. The Education Boards should pay special attention to making policies and on research. At present, these Boards are just a medium of conducting examinations. This is not enough. They should do much more than this. It has also been seen that many examinations conducted by the University Grants Commission (UGC) are being organized by the CBSE.

There is no need for this. The administration needs to look into this. The re-organization of Institutes and their proper administration is essential. If this is not done, resources will be misused and wasted.

Education plays an important role in the development of a person, family, society and nation. If we give the right education to our children, then only will we develop eligible and skilled human resources. Education helps the country in making an environment of research and innovation. Education brings out the personality, behavior and values of its citizens and helps them to become world-class citizens. That is why all countries try to make efforts to improve educational standards.

In India also much efforts have been made to improve educational standards. Otherwise also India has been known for its education system. India that was at the forefront of knowledge and science, studies and teaching was defeated by foreign invaders and was left behind in the field of education. After getting independence, we started working again in order to improve the education system.

With the view of making an improvement in education, the Mudaliar Committee was constituted. After this came the Kothari Commission. In 1986 the first Fundamental National Education Policy came into existence. In 1992 various amendments were made to it. 25 years have passed since then. During this period India has seen many social, cultural, economic and technical changes. It is essential that seeing these extensive changes, there should be fundamental changes in educational values and the educational machinery. We will have to reconsider our national education policy if we have to cater to the needs of the vast population with regard to education, innovation and research and to fulfill their expectations. This is an ongoing effort and that is why we should all become a part of this, so that it can be developed by mutual consent and deliberation.

Directions need to be determined with regard to the construction of educational institutes. Many people and organizations are opening and running schools with the sole purpose of making money. They are running schools with a business viewpoint. Because of their wrong viewpoint many schools that are equipped with the most modern facilities are becoming centers of anarchy. These schools create a hole in the pockets of the students' guardians with some excuse or the other. They are somehow pursuing the work of running their businesses under the garb of schools. Neither are they worried about the quality of education that they are imparting, nor about their security.

It is unfortunate that even schools are not secure places. Not only in schools that have a lack of resources, but even in those which are well equipped with all resources and amenities, various types of immoral and criminal activities are being carried out. These criminal activities that regularly take place in these schools keep on making the headlines of newspapers. Why this is happening needs to be looked into. This is not merely a problem connected with law and order. This situation has arisen because of the fall in moral values. Because of the faulty policy of keeping money and self at the top are the reasons why such type of violence, anarchy and immorality is rising in the society.

Seeing the bad situation of value-based education in the country it is difficult to believe that this is the same India where there used to be famous universities like Takshila and Nalanda. It is an irony that in the land that has been the work place of great souls like Buddha, Mahavir, Nanak, Kabir, Chanakya and Ramkrishna Paramhans, and who have moulded great talents, kings and scholars, education and teachers have reached this pitiable level. Today, teachers have forgotten their objectives and students have adopted the culture of showing a thumb as opposed to cutting off their thumbs and sacrificing it for their teachers.

India can be a role model for the world

By keeping in mind the philosophy of 'Vasudev Kutumbukam', India has always worked for the benefit of the entire world. This role of India is often denied because of historical reasons. It is important that we should have self-confidence in the good work that we do. When we ourselves do not have any knowledge of our past and qualities, what will we tell the world about it and how. Many countries of the world and the entire Asian region have been taking advantage of Indian knowledge, skill and its economy since thousands of years. Today many such countries are looking down at us who were grateful to us some time back.

The threat that China is making is the same China that was saved from a great epidemic because of an Indian guru– Bodhidharman. Such a great physician was given the status of God by the people of China because of his invaluable contribution, but most Indians must not have heard his name. During the first and second world wars the condition of China was extremely pitiable and it was a victim of many epidemics and famines. At that time, India had been China's largest benefactor. Indian physicians put their lives at stake and freed the Chinese of many infectious diseases. We have ourselves forgotten our works and that is why the world is also ignorant about our best works.

It is unfortunate that the same knowledge is being taken and weapons are being made and we are being made weak. The proposal to accept the privatization of education could prove to be dangerous for India. This will give rise to commercialism and the competition to earn more money. In order to imbue education with moral values and useful for the people, all organs of society will have to work together. It is essential that Indian citizens never forget their glorious and unique past. We need to tell the entire world of our achievements because the modern world does not believe in research and often takes claims to be true.

Education should be such that not only does it make the Indian citizens aware of their best qualities and history, but also makes the entire world aware of it. Education should be made free of all types of narrow views. Some elements are deliberately making efforts in the wrong direction. The dark hole of radicalism and 'jehad' is being watered and fed. We need to identify such elements. The entire world should be made aware of them. This violence and radicalism is the most prevalent in Central-Asia. The role of Saudi Arabia is often out under the scanner. The Madrasas all over the world and most of the religious educational institutions are given assistance from Saudi Arabia. Here, children are inculcated with the toxin of radicalism. An environment of hatred towards other religions and doctrines is developed here.

Fascist education and 'jihadi' mentality has developed this thinking among the new generation that a thought process that is different from the practices taught by Islam is bad and should be viewed with contempt. This feeling inspires them to look at other doctrines with hatred and to commit heinous and barbaric crimes against them. Islamic fascists have committed crimes against people of other religions on a large scale. They have been beheaded. Their women and children have been raped and heinous crimes committed against them. Iraq, Syria, Turkey, and the entire Central Asia and Bangladesh, Afghanistan, Pakistan etc are the victims of Islamic fascists. Here the creeper of fascism is flourishing and it has cursed the entire world to face the terrible conditions of terrorism.

In countries like Pakistan, the citizens are given a dose of fascism from childhood itself that the symbols of a 'sanatan' culture, that is, India and Hindus are enemies of Allah and they have no right to live. Islamic residents are made to take a pledge that they will establish Islamic rule by beheading the disbelievers of Islam or by committing suicide. They are told that it is their religious duty. By murdering the others, they will attain heaven and 'hoors' (heavenly angels).

In reality, fascism is an endless vicious cycle that is being strengthened by Pakistan, Saudi Arab and other Muslim countries. World super powers like America are nourishing these fascists for their own personal gains. A big part of the blame for the manner in which terrorism is making its presence felt lies at the feet of the world's super powers. America has recently concluded a pact of trillions of dollars of chemical warfare.

America has been giving support to Saudi Arab for the past many decades in order to keep its control over Asia and the Middle East and to keep its strategic position strong there. It is because of American support that many terrorist organizations have taken birth so that American interests are protected in the entire Asia and Middle East. Even today, instead of putting an end to terrorism in countries like Syria, Iran, Iraq, Palestine and North Korea, it is bent on establishing governments that will nurture it. While doing this it does not pay attention that because of its efforts the Islamic State and other radical organizations are becoming stronger with all types of resources, arms and money power. The refuge of terrorists-Pakistan- also gets the huge support from America. It is because of the large scale support and assistance of the super powers that terrorist organizations are making the roots of jihadi radicalism stronger and stronger all over the world.

Today, terrorist organizations are propounding Islam in a manner that they wish to. They even proclaim the liberal and progressive view of Islam to be inappropriate and doubtful. They dislike the Shias and other liberal Muslim communities and are violent towards them. For the terror organization of IS, the Islam of Saudi Arab is not according to the Islam that they propound. Along with Infidel (kaafir) States like India, Saudi Arab and its royal family is also the target of the IS.

'My Islam is nearer to Khuda than your Islam' this competition has become dangerous for the world. After the second World war, it was America that nurtured Islamic Jehad in order to put an end to the terror of communism. This creeper that was nurtured is responsible for the terror that the entire world has been subject to and is being forced to endure.

Along with terrorism India is the victim of many domestic and regional problems. Problems like Separatism, Regionalism and Naxalism create serious problems for the Indian law and order system. There is no doubt that Naxalism needs to be rooted out in order to establish peace in India. In areas where the pace of development cannot be speeded up, there special attention should be paid so that the citizens get proper opportunities to move ahead in life. The forces of Naxalism can be defeated by strengthening the process of development. Where required, force should be used. With the new policy, a lot has been achieved in this direction. There has been a speeding up of the process of surrender among the Naxals.

The youth who have been mislead by the Naxal organizations need to be made aware of nationalist ideas once again. Efforts should be made to train and educate them and bring them into the mainstream. The governments of many states are making creative efforts in this direction. In some States those youth who leave the Naxal organizations are given financial assistance. They are also given the benefit of government programs. If after surrendering someone wants to reverse the process of sterilization that he is made to undergo after being inculcated into Naxalism, it is done at the cost of the government. On surrendering the members of the Central Committee and the 'Polit Bureau' are given an amount of one crore rupees and those from smaller cadres are given one lakh rupee. And if someone surrenders along with arms, the amount has been increased.

The young generation should be given an opportunity to work. In many States because of the lack of employment anti national organizations are being successful in luring the youth. The government should make a scheme and provide employment to those Naxalites who surrender. In some states efforts are being made in this direction. They are being trained in three-month courses. In this duration they are also given an allowance of four thousand rupees every month. They are being given agricultural land and houses. Seeing their educational qualifications they are also given jobs. After surrendering, they are given the benefit of the food scheme, health insurance scheme and all other government schemes. The cases that are pending in courts against the naxals need to be speeded up. Till three years ago the naxals who surrendered did not get all government facilities. Good behavior was not a basis for jobs and other provisions. There has been a change after the inclusion of employment opportunities. The amount of money after surrender by a Naxal has been increased 20 times. It is necessary that the youth that has lost direction due to other reasons like unemployment, inequality, injustice and poverty should be brought into the mainstream. This energy should be utilized in works like nation building.

No doubt India is plagued with thousand of problems. We have that capability and courage to tide over our problems. If we become strong, capable and united internally, we can become capable of giving direction and guidance to the entire world. It is the responsibility of each Indian that he make his contribution to this objective.

The increasing tension due to consumerism

Life is becoming stressful and violent due to modern consumerism and the fall in values. Such situations affect the most capable and successful people. Many successful and influential people end up taking their own lives. Many top bureaucrats and district officials are sometimes compelled to take their own lives. We should look for the reasons in our societal life.

Mukesh Pandey who was the DM of Buxar district of Bihar was a simple and uncomplicated man. His achievement of getting the 14th rank in the Civil Services shows that he was a meritorious person, but he gave up his life because of some personal reasons by coming under a train. Before committing suicide he made a video where he shared his problem. This person was very unhappy because of some domestic problems. He had said in the video, "Excess of everything is bad." A person who is fed up of the daily fights and quarrels sees suicide as the only way out. A cultured society should understand his problems, but also find a solution to them. It is surprising that we are becoming irresponsible in understanding the feelings of other people. Without giving it proper thought many people started calling Mukesh Pandey a weak and cowardly person. Nobody thought it necessary to understand why this person who was part of the country's topmost administrative service took such a decision. It is often being seen in Indian families that the condition of men is becoming very complex and complicated.

The most worrying situation in family quarrels and struggles is that of men. Generally the condition of men is the most pitiable when daily quarrels take place between his wife and parents. If he takes the side of his wife, the society is quick to brand him a 'joru ka gulam' and if he takes the side of his parents then he is compelled to hear the sarcastic comments from his wife. There is no doubt that emotionally the men have to bear the brunt of the situation. Women lighten their hearts by crying, but where does the poor man go? It is not necessary that every time the women is the victim. Along with women, men also have to make a lot of sacrifices. Perhaps they cannot tell us by beating the drums. Before making any judgement we should try and understand the situation properly. One should not make statements against a person without thinking.

Actually we have no right to call that person a coward, about whose mental and emotional state we have no idea. Men and women are both equal in society and their feelings should be understood with emotions and sensibility. The contribution of men to the working of the house is not less. When men and women work shoulder to shoulder in running the house, the society should not raise a finger at one person. We need to make a proper evaluation of the circumstances and try to help the families or troubled people.

Suicides and crimes by such talented and highly educated men of the society is an immense loss to the entire country.

In such cases the rest of the members of the family should display some understanding. Instead of increasing the tension they should try and establish a balance. Whenever such situations arise, family members should try to normalize things. Generally we do not talk much on these topics and try to avoid them.

This is not right. People who are undergoing such situations and stress should talk about their problems with those close to them. This helps in finding a solution. Without reinstating Yoga, spirituality and 'satsang' in Indian society the best of moral values cannot be propagated. When a feeling of purity in thought and service and sacrifice is developed the society will automatically develop as a healthy and well-organized society.

6

Unnecessary imitation of the West

Today, we imitate the West in all spheres of life. It is surprising that we do not imbibe the good qualities and the ethos of a work-oriented society from them; instead we imitate them in spheres where we are better than them since times immemorial. We have even forgotten that our contribution in the fields of philosophy, spirituality, arts, culture and civilization has been far more than the West and far more extensive.

Indian Art and Culture has always been providing guidance to the entire world. It was in India that cultural revolutions in fields such as classical music, singing, dance, acting and dance forms first began. Today we are looking towards the West in the fields such as Arts and culture. We have to develop our original Indian Art. The history of Indian art and culture has been glorious. We have to take our heritage forward. Cinema and television can play an important role in it. These mediums of information and broadcasting should be properly utilized.

Restricting the use of a powerful medium like cinema to the acquisition of money and to entertain would be an insult to this medium. Cinema can play a much bigger role than this. The citizens of the country can be trained and educated through this medium. It has been seen that the work that could not be done through educational institutes, government schemes and various campaigns was easily achieved through the medium of cinema.

Recently many such films have been successfully screened which have not only given the citizens an opportunity to understand various issues, but they have also understood their role and responsibility towards some serious issues. Films like 'Toilet', 'Dangal', 'Newton', 'Secret Superstar', 'Taare Zameen Par' and Three idiots" have done the work of changing the mindsets of people. Such efforts should be appreciated.

There was a time when films that gave a message were considered to be serious and art films and there was a very limited and well-off section of society that viewed them. A majority of the country's population could not develop their understanding of such serious films. This situation is now changing. The average person is developing an understanding of the country's problems and the solutions. Artists and enlightened people of society should develop these mediums and should emphasize on it in the backdrop of the needs and requirements of the country. It is a good omen that films that are made on good topics and that give a good message to society are being successful from a commercial angle also.

It is correct that the success of a film is gauged from the amount of money that it earns. Its success depends on the number of crores that it garners and if lags behind on the basis of figures it is declared a flop. The Media in our country also focuses too much on commercial figures. Art should not be looked at from a commercial angle only. Its success should not just depend on how much it sold and earned but other facets should also be taken into consideration. It is more important to see what effect the film had on the society and people. How much people debated on the issues raised in the film should also matter.

But if the objective of the film is to be commercially successful, it is not a bad thing. The careers of many people are connected to it. Earning money can be one objective, but not the only objective. Normally it is said that film production is a sort of business. So money plays a big part in it. But if making money is the sole objective there are many other businesses where money can be made. The process of film production is a creative and artistic subject. Its creative aspect should be the main focus. Economic benefits should be secondary.

In recent years films are giving rise to controversies too. Questions are raised on the role of the Censor Board also. Cases of bribes being paid to members of the Film Censor Board also keep surfacing. Such cases bring a bad name to a creative field like cinema. It is essential that creative and talented people enter the film industry in large numbers. Youth who are keen to make creative message-centric films should be given special assistance and protection by the government. An institute like the Film Censor Board should have eligible and capable people in it. In a creative and artistic field like this the amount of commercial gains and political interference should be minimized.

The work that belongs to the Censor Board or the Film Certification and Appellate Tribunal cannot be left to the people who start opposing it because of political reasons or a narrow mentality without even seeing it. If there is something that is objectionable in a film it should be opposed in a democratic and constitutional manner. If something objectionable is found after the exhibition of the film the doors of the judiciary can be knocked upon. It is inappropriate to oppose a film or a book or any other medium of art by the use of force. This usually happens because of political reasons. We need to stop such tendencies in India. If it is not stopped, then it will become a permanent tendency for such people to react in such a manner towards all creative works.

In this modern age of the technological revolution there are various media for information, entertainment and transmission. Three decades ago the radio was the only means of entertainment, information and broadcasting. Even after so many decades some programs of 'Akashvani' are still etched in the memories of people. Many people still prefer 'Akashvani' to other modes. 'Akashvani' has had a special and memorable journey. It was around 1924 that some radio clubs had started transmission, but because of financial crunches they could not last long. After this the Indian Broadcasting Company began transmitting its radio programs in Bombay from 23rd July 1027.

On 26th August 1927 regular transmission started from Kolkata also. While inaugurating the radio transmission the then Viceroy Lord Irwin had said that it would certainly prove to be a boon for Indians in the future. Although this forecast did not prove to be true because the Indian Broadcasting Company became bankrupt by 1930. After that the British government constitute the 'Indian State Broadcasting Service'. At that time the radio services were under the labor Ministry from an administrative viewpoint.

From 1936 government radio transmission came to be known as 'Akashvani' all over the country. At that time three objectives were determined for radio- Information, education and entertainment. Even today these main objectives have not changed. In reality any transmission medium should fulfill these three objectives. At the time that 'Akashvani' began its operations, India was a poor, and socially diverse country. Educating people and creating awareness in a poor and illiterate country was a big responsibility. India's geographic and social diversity was a complex challenge. Between 1930 and 1936 two news bulletins were transmitted from Mumbai and Kolkata. Those days news was not taken from any agency, instead the news- readers used to read out the main news from the day's newspapers.

After the constitution of the Central News Institute in 1935, there was a proper development of news bulletins. In 1951 the development of the radio was included in the Five Year plan. After this, Aksashvani never looked back. It included all sections of society in its family. The history of Akashvani's popularity was created when the 'Vividh Bharti Sewa' was started on 3rd October 1957. In a very short while the listeners choice songs program was being echoed in all houses. Programs like 'Filmi kalakaron se mulakaat', 'Jaimala' for the soldiers 'Hawa Mahal' and other programs became a part of people's lives.

In this enchanting and historic voyage of transmission radio achieved many milestones of success. The name Akashvani is known all over the world. Its introductory tune is also unique, with which the transmission began in many centers. Although many centers now transmit programs all 24 hours, therefore one does not hear the introductory tune there. The transmission of 'Vivid Bharti' is also for all 24 hours so this tune is not played there also. This inimitable tune was composed by the music department of the 'Indian Broadcasting Company' in 1936 by an official by the name of Walter Koffman.

The voice waves of Akashvani echo not only in India, but also in foreign countries. After independence, the first prime minister of India, Pandit Jawaharlal Nehru had given his famous 'Tryst with Destiny' speech in the interview taken in Parliament, and it was heard by the people through the medium of Akashvani. Today, prime minister, Narendra Modi's program, 'Mann Ki Baat' is transmitted through the same medium. This program has again connected the people of the country to Akashvani and Radio. Prime Minster Narendra Modi has increased the TRP of Akashvani many fold. There is no doubt that 'Mann Ki Baat' has proved economically beneficial for Akashvani.

Today the reach of radio is almost 98%. In the technical era of the 21st century, Akashvani has changed itself. Under it Local Frequency Modulation, or FM centers have come up with great speed. This has increased the qualitative level of the programs. Today, there are many FM channels that are entertaining the people and enriching the tradition of radio.

In 1976 programs sponsored by Vividh Bharti began, and the popularity of radio reached its peak. Amin Sayani's 'Binaca Geet Mala' is still an evergreen part of our memories. Man set foot on the Moon on 23rd July 1968 and on the same day Delhi Akashvani began 'Yuvvani'. Keeping the invaluable tradition of classical music and folk music alive and popularizing it has been another achievement of Akashvani. Many important composers, scholars of classical music, writers and journalists have been connected to Akashvani.

Akashvani has safely kept the interviews of talented people from the field of Indian literature, cinema and arts with it. In various programs like Jaimala, interviews with well-known people are regularly transmitted by Akashvani. There is no doubt that these recordings are invaluable cultural heritage of India. The museum of Akashvani is one of the most unique museums in the world. Even today there are some priceless recordings present in the museum. The interviews and creative writings of Mahadevi Verma, Jaishankar Prasad, Nirala, Bacchan ji, Ramnath Awasthi, Ramdhari Singh Dinkar, Sahir Ludhianvi, Shakeel Badayuni and others are India's great heritage. All these priceless creations are available in Akashvani's library. Now they are available in the form of CD's also.

Every morning 'Vandana', 'Bhajans' and the transmission of Ramcharitmanas; old hindi film songs and songs based on Ragas, programs for the ladies in the afternoon, youth programs like 'Yuvvani' and others like 'Hawa Mahal', 'Chaya Geet', etc used to provide us with so much relaxation, pleasure and spiritual experiences that the programs that are transmitted through so many channels and social media these days, cannot provide. The influence and quality that Indian radio has had cannot be found anywhere else. The quality and popularity of Indian radio has even surprised the western world. Indian all India Radio and other services are seen as inspirational by all countries of the world. It is unfortunate that today Indian radio and TV copy the lowly programs of western countries and produce and transmit their Indian versions.

Like Radio and TV Indian cinema also seems to be very influenced by Hollywood. Our artists make all possible efforts to join the race of the Oscars. We need to free ourselves from such feelings that our talent should be gauged by the west. The quality of our work should no doubt be world class, but to expect a certificate from the west for everything will be mental slavery and a vacuum of thoughts. Indian cinema does not need any certification from anyone. The best social and educational movies have been made in India since 1930s. This system continues till today. Now Indian films are being seen internationally and being acclaimed. The business of the Indian Film Industry is increasing at a global level.

The mark of Indian cinema can be seen in the entire world today. After Hollywood the Indian Film Industry is the biggest entertainment industry today. This powerful medium needs to be aware of its social responsibilities also. The objective of the film industry should not be limited to earning money. That is possible in other businesses also. Cinema is an artistic medium. It has a responsibility towards the society and nation. It cannot be set free from this responsibility.

Today the success of a film depends on the amount it grosses. It is given a certificate based on the crores that it has earned and if it fails on the basis of figures it is considered useless. The Media also mostly talks about a film's earnings. The decision of its success should not be only on how much it ran but also on other facets.

The influence of a film should be seen and judged by how much the society and people liked it, how much people talked about the issues raised by it. But the monetary aspect is important because the livelihoods of many people are connected to films.

Normally it is said that film-making is a type of business. But is different from other businesses in many aspects. If making money was the only one then there are many other businesses that give a much better return on money-they have the ability to give more returns in the same time frame and with the same investment, but if people are in the business of film making their main objectives have to include giving the right message to society and making people aware of issues.

In recent times, many films have created controversies. In India questions are raised about the film certification board. Controversies like bribe giving and ideological agendas are some of them. Indian society is often seen embroiled in useless debates about the exhibition of films because of political reasons. A lot of hullabaloo is created regarding some films so that one can garner political headlines and become a part of the news.

Many times the producers and actors connected with a film also try to create controversies so that they can gain free publicity from it. All these things are not appropriate and are just narrow efforts at earning profits at the cost of the society and nation. Such efforts need to be strictly curbed. For this the society also needs to become mature and aware. Indian society cannot be such weak and immature that it can be swayed by a film of a mere two to two and half hours.

It is unfortunate that often some anti-social elements and political outfits try and raise such unnecessary debates; this is done to divert the attention of the people and society from fundamental issues and go towards suspect issues.

Like cinema, literature also does the work of giving a direction to society. Literature is basically a mirror of society. If society and life need to be given a proper direction, then literature and creativity also need to go in the right direction. It also directly affects literary creativity. In this age of news revolution, the entire world has transformed itself into a global village. Literature is becoming dependent on new means of information technology. This also has its own modulatory benefits and limits. Another extensive benefit is that there is no delay in making things available to the people.

The new revolution has had an important role in changing the entire form of literary creativity. Contrary to the traditional method, writers now have various media to express their thoughts. They have their own blogs. Many have their own websites. These media have changed the relationship between writer and reader. Now writings are published on 'Facebook' and debates take place on them. There has been an increase in the readership of Hindi literature. Besides poems and stories and novels, subjects like science, technology, environment and media are also being written about a lot.

In the Book fairs that are organized all over the country and abroad, besides books on literature, books on other topics are also being sold on a large scale. Writings on the lives of people are increasing. Now a big portion of writing is not limited to biographic but has become connected to the objective of self-help. Newspapers, magazines, electronic media, blogs, social media, films, cinema, TV, radio and other mediums are increasingly being used for the publishing and transmission of self-help books. Intellectual and literary debates are not restricted to intellectuals. In the entire country seminars, workshops, conclaves, etc are organized on a regular basis. Debates are moving away from the precincts of professorial academics. This has broken many superstitions and traditional beliefs and the sphere of literature and publishing has widened greatly. Many such subjects that literary writers and authors used to consider as second grade are not only acceptable today, but are widely popular. Today's young writer does not consider mainstream films to be untouchable or B-grade. He does not consider film music as banned and does not flinch from their socialism. Perhaps this is the reason that an extensive range for Hindi intellectual debate is being created. Today's author does not consider the writings in other languages to be castaways, instead he takes inspiration from them. He is also making the popular English literature a source of his inspiration.

In order for literature to be more useful and profitable for society, the government and Sahitya Academy will have to fulfill its role and responsibility in a more alert manner. Many times it is said that the above two institutions are not fulfilling their role properly. The criticism and praise of the Sahitya Academy's are often not based on facts and do not list out the positive and negative qualities. Preconditioned notions are also clearly seen. We need to make a real and factual evaluation. Instead of encouraging and refining them, government institutions often end up in creating obstacles in their development.

A culture of reading and learning needs to be developed

For a very long time most institutes in India are known to be major hubs of selfish interests, passive elements and a formless bureaucracy. There has also been the belief that benefits can be attained from these institutes without making too much effort and without having any special capabilities. This situation is slowly changing. It is very important that capable and prestigious people be appointed to such high and responsible posts. Without doing this no institute connected with people's welfare can obtain its objectives.

The intelligent section of society in the country also demands that the government should not interfere in social, human and linguistic education and culture and social and creative activities. This entire sphere should be a subject of society's own creativity and thinking. This responsibility will have to be borne by the society. Without this it will always prove to be politically motivated, quality-less and meaningless. For a culture of reading to be established in the country this society will have to become a literature and art loving. For this the administration will have to come forward. For the country to be cultured and knowledgeable about all things, a library culture will need to be developed.

A law should be made to ensure that in the manner that a house has rooms, kitchen and bathrooms, similarly there should be a study room and a library too. The design of a house should be passed only when it has a library and a study room. It is surprising that countries with a population of just one-two crores publish four times more books than a country like India with 130 crore citizens. This unfortunate situation should change soon. If the Indian society has to become addicted to something, it should be books and literature.

Literature has been surrounded by various forms of bad practices. These practices also need to be changed. When a creator becomes a follower of power, there arise distortions in literature. An author will have to wield his pen without fear and by keeping justice in mind, if he has to contribute towards making a good society. Many of today's authors are not concerned about creativity, but are more concerned with getting awards. The new generation of writers needs to beware of this tendency. After globalization, the correct future path of the independence of the country can only be an evaluation of the ruling powers and new tendencies of society, and literature based on this. Till the time we do not reflect the truths and needs in our writings, literature cannot equip us for life's journey.

Indian culture is well known for its uniqueness the world over. India is the only culture in the world where a person's life has been divided into four periods and stages. India has become a world leader on this basis. Till the time the Indian economy does not re-organize itself according to these four stages, the welfare of India and the world will not be possible. India will not gain by emulating western countries. India should give momentum to its development programs on the basis of its fundamental viewpoint and environmental factors.

India is being deprived of its fundamental knowledge and uniqueness by coming under western influence. We destroy our fundamental and contextual ideologies without thinking and becoming slaves to the materialistic culture that benefits the west. We have even forgotten that India has had its own fundamental research and proven knowledge in the spheres of art and culture and health and medicine. We have forgotten that Ayurveda has been a fundamental and special knowledge of India. The entire world has been looking at it with awe and wonder since ancient times.

Neglecting Indian fundamental knowledge

Because of the increasing pollution and tensions yoga and Ayurved have become necessities of life. We need to develop and encourage our fundamental knowledge and Ayurveda from a new angle. We need to connect the ancient knowledge of Ayurved with modern equipment and technology. Ayurved took birth many thousands of years ago on Indian land. The Rishis and Munis made this medical system accessible to the people. Compared to English medicines, Ayurved is an ancient system.

The word 'Ayurved' is made up of two Sanskrit words. 'Ayu' which means 'Life' and 'Ved' which means 'Knowledge'. It is believed that Ayurved took birth in India 5000 years ago and at that time its knowledge was available only orally.

The first written evidence about the Ayurvedas is found in the Vedas. In the Atharveda, there is reference to the Ayurveda system of medicine in the form of 114 Shlokas and Mantras. 'Charak-Sanhita', that was written about 2000 years back, 'Sushruta Sanhita' and 'Ashtang Hridaya' are considered to be the first three ancient texts on Ayurveda.

It is believed that Rishi Dhanvantri had obtained the knowledge of Ayurveda from God Brahma. He is called the God of Ayurveda. The Central 'Ayush' Ministry celebrates Dhanvantri Trayodashi or Dhanteras as the day of Ayurveda. Ayurveda is based on Ayurvedic plants, 'jadi-bootis' and many other ancient elements, that is why it has no ill effect on the body. Not only does it remove the symptoms of the disease, but hits at the root of the problem. Compared to Allopathy the Ayurveda medicines are cheaper because it is free of harmful chemicals. Most of the medicines can be prepared at home. Yoga is also a big part of Ayurveda. This system not only works on the body but also on the mind. People can make a few changes in their lifestyle and can cure themselves of diseases.

In the Indian lifestyle we can gather adequate medicines from nature itself. Some decades ago Indian families used to remain healthy by making use of various products that are available in homes. There used to be various Ayurvedic medicines available in all Indian homes. There was 'Ajwain' for reducing weight, 'Ashwgandha' for reducing tension and depression, 'Brahmi' for the brain and the nervous system, 'Elaichi' as a digestive,

'Jeera' for improving the digestive system, 'Mulethi' for relief from swelling, 'Manjitha' for purifying the blood, 'Neem' for detoxifying the body and increasing blood circulation and 'Haldi' for enriching the skin. All these things are essential elements in an Indian kitchen. Today we are forgetting our basic knowledge because of the influence of the West. The society and government need to come together to keep the Indian system of medicine alive.

7

Be human being first

We should not become very enamoured of our materialistic achievements and resources. When our time is good, we need to be aware of it. This is the time when we should think in the proper direction and ponder that if God and Nature are giving success to a person, it can be the result of his good deeds. If we start becoming proud, greedy, lustful etc in our good time, it will eclipse the actual purpose of the reward. We should make proper use of the achievements. In reality, whatever man gets, is for distributing it in society.

The all-powerful Nature also gives us this message. Even though the sun, moon, earth, atmosphere, sky etc are all powerful, they have been continuing to do their work with all discipline since times immemorial. If these natural forces stop working even for a moment, the world will come to an end. Despite having incomparable strength these powers do not become arrogant like humans. Rivers have not put a restriction on the use of their waters, air has not put it on its flow, and the moon does not hesitate to give its light. Perhaps it is because of this that it has been happening since times immemorial and the stock of these sources has not come to an end. When the mind rises above distortions, and learns to live under the power of God, that is the time when he develops the quality of forbearance.

We should always remember that tolerance is not cowardice or escapism. Being tolerant is a quality in itself. Overcoming one's defects is in itself a feat that is incomparably courageous. The person who has established a victory over his mind and senses is the one who has established a victory in this world and creation. Man has not taken birth in order to establish his rule on this earth. If he has to establish his rule anywhere, it should be over his own body, mind and consciousness. The objective of his birth is to be under the protection of God and cleanse his soul by washing away all his sins. Happiness lies in the pursuit of this.

Nature has endowed man with various types of powers and resources. We should always make good use of these resources given to us. Nature has also bestowed us with a mind capable of thinking and a voice. Actually voice is a very difficult achievement. It is also representative of power and energy. Whether it will become a curse or a blessing depends on its use. If voice is used in a controlled manner, it can be a great weapon for a person, society and for creation. But its misuse leads to a lot of problems in human life.

Word and voice have their own uniqueness. The manner of speaking affects the result of a work. Since ancient times, wise men have given us the message that our voice should be modulated and thoughtful. The same thing can be said in an aggressive tone and in a calm and decent manner. Sometimes even if a harsh truth is said with discretion, it proves beneficial. Words do have their effect, but more than words the meaning that is conveyed has an effect. A balanced outlook makes us realize that we should use our words with a lot of caution and thinking.

Man is a thinking and intelligent being. His wisdom and his intelligence should be reflected in the choice of his words. A man has many emotions. If there is greed, there is satisfaction also. If he has awareness about his affairs, he also has feelings of sacrifice and balance. A man should be compassionate, liberal and should be aware of the welfare of others. He should always keep the objective of 'Vasudev Kutumbakam' in mind and not be violent towards any body. A simple life and spiritual development gives inspiration to man to lead a meaningful life.

The life of great men is inspirational for the entire society. The words uttered by the best of mankind who have taken a vow for truth and purity are like a panacea for the welfare of people. The proper use of words and voice give rise to power, welfare and positivity, whereas its misuse gives rise to frustration, tension and anger. This creates a lot of mental and physical problems. We should always see that we use our voice in such a manner that it is beneficial for everyone. Voice and the energy that it creates should be helpful in establishing life-values, ideals and good behavior in our social and national life. When it becomes another name for Godliness only then can this priceless gift form God be made meaningful.

Man should always keep making efforts. There is no such work in this creation that is impossible for man to do. The question is only of his efforts. On the basis of work, normally three types of people are found in society. One are those who on hearing of some work immediately say that they will not be able to do it, and wait for someone else to do it. The second type are those who want to do the work and even start it, but as soon as they face some difficulty they give up, without knowing what the result will be. The third type of people are those who think about the various aspects of a work before starting it. After proper thinking about it when they ultimately take a decision to do it they do it in the proper manner and do not rest till they complete it. These are the best type of people. No work should be left unfinished and no work should be begun without proper deliberation. A well thought out and logical work can be taken to its final conclusion on the basis of hard work.

A person should never take such a decision in his life for which he will repent in the future. That is why before taking any decision, he should think about all the alternatives and keep all good advice in mind. There is no need to doubt the advice taken from eligible people. With constant deliberation and discussions with eligible people our decision making capacity and level of our decision goes up.

However be the business of the modern age, each person should do some creative work on the basis of his capability and save time and energy. Getting some free time is very essential in the busy schedule of our lives. Man should rid himself of all types of tensions and clashes of opinions from time to time and spend some time in meditation and creativity.

He should take some leave and make a move towards creativity. Free time helps a person's creativity to take wings and fly.

The good works that are done by us can help us obtaining happiness. No work is actually big or small. The importance of a work lies behind its meaning. The work that is associated with a good objective does not remain a work and becomes a prayer. We have to work every minute of our life. We cannot remain without working for a single moment. When we have to work, then why not do the best and sacred works. If we do not have spiritual knowledge and moral strength, we will not have been able to keep our work on the good path, despite having all the skills and capability at our disposal.

We get this to know which work or path is best for us through spiritual knowledge and good company. The person who works in his field with honesty and dedication is never unsuccessful in life. Such people achieve all their objectives.

Politics should become people's policies

Every person has an important role in the creation of the society and the country. In a country where about 65% of the population is young, there the possibility of success of such an endeavor increases. We have to take society out of that mentality which says that 'Nothing can be done' and 'After all what can we do?'. All political organizations should understand that their existence and the existence of the democracy is possible only when the people have faith in them. The existence of both can be in jeopardy because of the increasing problems and in the absence of no system to redress them. That is why we have to rise above narrow caste based politics and organize ourselves to achieve our objectives.

The objective of politics should not and cannot be for personal gain. And it should not be the for obtaining power. All these objectives are small and an insult to political values. The eventual aim of politics should be the creation of nation and society. Those people who cannot dedicate their lives and their all for the achievement of this grand objective should be kept away from politics. The day that such ideal political values are established in India, will be the day when we will start moving in the direction of becoming the greatest country of this world. India is a vast country. We are not making proper use of our incomparable human resources of 125 crore people. If 250 crore hands are used for some task, then nothing is impossible in this world. The vast population of the country needs to be organized and its energy channeled on a definite and clear objective, only then will the population become its strength and will be capable of taking it to any height.

A man should work without thinking of the fruits of his work. This is what has been taught to him since times immemorial. This has been a tradition in this land of India that is the land of the 'Gita'. It is not easy to understand this philosophy of being a 'Karmyogi'. For this a person needs to walk on the path of self-analysis and goodness. In reality a work is regarded as having been successfully done when the desired results are obtained. A person who is doing his work with dedication always has his eyes on the objective.

The pleasure that will be obtained from the achievement lies in its womb and cannot be seen. That is why it appears so enchanting in our imagination. The desire to obtain that objective becomes stronger. A man is ready to do the hardest of tasks in order to achieve his objective. It seems as if his life is incomplete without achieving his desires. He creates a dream world–that is life will change after obtaining his objective and he will be showered in happiness. This makes him ignore his present. A man does not get any pleasure from that work from which he has expectations.

Every man wants to make progress while leading an upwardly mobile life. Making progress in life is man's basic nature. Progress is not possible without hard work and efforts. A man has to work as hard as his objectives are. These efforts lead to an increase in a man's capacity, which cannot be taken away by anyone. A man should always make efforts in the direction of his soul's welfare. There is actually no work in this creation more important for our welfare than that we keep on bettering and improving ourselves. We should always think about our spiritual upliftment. The efforts made in this direction are the actual deeds that we should do. By doing this, a man's self-respect becomes more in his own eyes and that becomes permanent. Outward achievements raise us in the eyes of others, which is temporary.

There is no material achievement or respect that is worth obtaining, that has not been obtained before us by lakhs of successful people. If such innumerable achievements are limited to nourishing the body and sensory happiness, they get destroyed with the destruction of man's physical body. We can eat the best food, and wear the most expensive clothes or use the most expensive products but they have no meaning if we are not able to uplift ourselves spiritually, morally and internally.

The actors of yesteryears are not worth remembering because of their temporary achievements. The society considers those worth emulating who dedicate their lives to the upliftment and welfare of human life. When a man focuses his attention on the present and in doing so experiences pleasure in what he is doing, this no doubt increases the quality of his work. His objective also becomes easier. The work ethics of the Gita gives us this same inspiration.

It was because of their great qualities that despite being poor and penniless, the entire society considered them as ideals and took their lives as inspiration and turned their lives towards their own welfare. This is a proven fact that if we have qualities and abilities, the rest of the achievements come on their own. Objectives are necessary to give a direction to one's efforts, but honest efforts have their own rewards. When we demean ourselves to achieve materialistic objectives and dirty our soul, then we might succeed in achieving our objective but because these are immoral we do not derive real pleasure and joy from them. It is necessary that we follow the path of truth and direct our energies towards the achievement of the highest objectives.

How to do nation's building

The responsibility of nation building lies on the shoulder of every citizen, but the prime task if of the policies and of politics. Politics should be directed towards the welfare of people. It should not be limited to the obtainment of power and resources. This is a widespread belief. It is an unfortunate truth that after independence Indian politics turned away from higher ideals and moral values. In the place of building society and the nation, politics became just a tool to obtain power in any which way. This situation is not at all auspicious for India.

A country that had been bearing the slavery of foreign invaders since thousands of years, if even after becoming independent it has been cursed to tolerate the selfish and divisive nature of political leadership, then the downfall of the country is certain. It is not that Independent India has not had eligible servants of the people, but their numbers and effects have been limited.

Today, there is a large number of such politicians who cheat the society and the people just to get hold of power, but also endanger the unity, secularism and security of the country.

The society has itself become divided amongst various castes, sections and sects because of the bad influence and behavior of such politicians. In the 21st century it is important for India that not only does it become free of such polluted politics, but should also compensate for the condition that the country has been reduced to because of bad politics. Politics should be imbued with such basic principles such as "simple living and high thinking". Till the time the behavior of politicians becomes impartial, transparent and selfless, the country will not get the right direction. If no improvement has been seen in the political and behavioral spheres, the citizenry is also responsible to an extent. The citizenry will have to play an active role for such a change to occur.

It is fortunate that the Indian society is being seen to accept the importance of eligible representatives of the people. The society, and especially the youth need to come out of the narrow confines of caste, religion and personal gains if we are to create a better India. There has never been a dearth of 'actors' in this country. There is no dearth of eligible, wise, talented and sacrificing people who are ready to sacrifice their personal gains without making a display of it and are doing such creative and unique work in society that was not possible even for big organizations and the government. If they are able to do this, it is because of their good behavior, sacrifice and hard work that the ordinary people stood behind him and was inspired to work alongside.

In Chattisgarh state and other 'Adivasi' areas, and some border areas of India, there are many such selfless people who have dedicated their entire lives to the service of the deprived societies without forming the headlines in the media. It is because of them that the society is still able to remain alive. There are so many IT engineers, administrators, scientists, environmentalists, industrialists, teachers and women in the country who have been working to give a creative direction to their regions through their efforts. We should all respect such capable and talented people. Their efforts should be brought to the notice of the society, so that everybody gets inspired and finds a direction.

It is surprising that even today real hard work does not get recognition in India. There is no tradition of any type of research or studies being conducted with regard to the works of real heroes that change the society. Indian society does not give any importance to the real heroes, leaving aside film stars, cricket players and politicians.

It is unfortunate that in our country people are aware of the average TV artists, and at the same time consider them their idols. Whereas, if some topmost scientist, philosopher, thinker, teacher or scholar is presented before the citizens of the country, very few people will have any knowledge about that person. Such type of behavior is an insult to talent. We tend to glorify the small things in life and belittle the important things. The best that is there in this world is not just what is shown on TV and published in newspapers.

It is a general concept that Indian society respects only those people through whom they can derive some benefit or those who are forcefully shoved down our throats through TV and other media. Indian English and electronic media that is full of Western music deliberately belittles Indian philosophy, and Indian traditional village culture on the strength of their wealth and advertising revenue. It is deliberately trying to create such a society in India that acclaims a materialistic culture and is a slave to it. It is for the creation of such a society that the Media and Newspapers are full of Hollywood news, useless gossip and entertainment oriented news. Such type of news and information is of no use to the Indian society. It is just a scheme of the multinational consumerist society that wants to divert the attention from the basic problems facing the country. India's welfare lies in discretionary spending and simplicity, where we display a tendency to consume only that much that meets man's minimum requirements.

Narrow political ideas have divided Indian society in the name of caste and religion. Candidates can be seen inciting speeches in the name of caste and religion in all the small and big elections. The Supreme Court has recently given a verdict that soliciting votes in the name of caste and religion will be considered inappropriate, but is the Election Commission able to impose any penalty on any candidate or party for violation of the Election Code of Conduct is a moot question. If someone violates the Code of Conduct, such behavior should be strictly condemned. In India the basic feeling behind absorbing the election code of conduct is missing and it is followed only in its technical aspect and that is the end of it. This outlook is taking India into the quagmire of politics.

The violation of the Election Code of Conduct and moral values is often not seriously taken in Indian politics. Many times Indian politicians violate the Code of Conduct in order to be in the headlines of the news. The reality is that in most cases of violation the Election Commission just sends notices. After some days an answer is sent to the notice and the matter ends there. In some cases the Commission registers a case. Many such cases have been dragging for years. That is why there is no use of registering a case.

The Commission cannot put a restriction on the candidate in a legal manner. If a person gives a speech from the side of a candidate or a party, then the Commission hardly does what it should do. It has got only one weapon. And that is cancelling the elections at a few chosen election constituencies, but this is the ultimate weapon. It can be used only occasionally. Besides inciting speeches, political parties often dole out free amenities in order to win elections. This is also immoral. It makes politics dirty and also makes the society passive. Such speeches promising freebies are noting but the misuse of public funds for narrow political gains.

The Supreme Court had asked the Election Commission to prepare directives in this regard, and it has been issued, but it is difficult to say whether the promises that the parties are making in the propaganda, are true or false. The Commission has asked the parties to give information about the source of these funds. True to habit, the political parties are ignoring these, but the election commission has no right to take any action against them. By changing the laws and giving the commission the right to take action can put a rein on these problems. Some elements do not like political improvements, they want the status quo to remain.

Political groups that take advantage of their money power and criminal elements see these changes as a threat. Some citizens also feel that if the commission makes some mistake, or it is accused of taking sides or its action is challenged in the Courts, the problem will escalate. Some people say that there should not be too many restrictions on freedom of expression. The electors should be made to decide on the basis of their discretion which party they want. The Election Commission is not an institute that makes laws or punishes the criminals. The Police and the Courts are there for this. The Commission can stop the candidates from canvassing and can also prevent their entry to some particular constituency.

Ultimately the final solution to the political improvements lies in the hands of the people themselves. When the people stop giving votes the to candidates with a bad impression, the problem will come to an end, but this will take a long time. In this age of social media, news reaches everywhere within the blinking of an eyelid. Today, the entire world has become a global village. The effect of technology has been widespread. Every person on this earth is connected to the newest forms of technology and transmission. These forms are misused too. Many untruths are propagated as rumors on social media. Even facts and pictures that have no relation to the incident are connected to it. Such things create disharmony, anarchy and violence.

Recently, rumors were fanned about some communal and caste violence because of the misuse of social media. Often the ordinary person does not have the time or the knowledge to separate the truth from the lies. The only method to fight lies is to bring out the truth. With regard to the rumors and lies transmitted through social media, some news channels, newspapers and citizen forums have conducted surveys to bring out the truth. Such commendable efforts should be given impetus so that people do not get caught in the net of lies and deceit. 'Satymev Jayate' has been the basic Mantra of the Indian administrative system and citizen life. We have to make all possible efforts to keep it unimpaired.

Topmost priority for public related natters

Indian politics should try and reach the pinnacle of intellectualism and sensitivity. Today, the best intellectual talent is coming forward in Indian politics. The level of intellectualism in the Parliament needs to be raised. All parties should deliberate upon it. The situation that the Parliament is in today is related to Indian democracy. There are many defects in Indian democracy. There cannot be extensive debates on the educational reforms and health programs in the political field.

Important topics like education, health, corruption, foreign policy, internal security cannot become the base of electoral politics. Even today, Indian politics is not able to rid itself from caste, religion and regional benefits. Democracy is an ideal ideology, but it will be helpful for society only when we are able to give it a covering of eligibility, intellectualism and equality. We do not need to look for an alternative to democracy by putting a light to the ideology of democracy.

Despite the many defects, democracy is a great idea. It is the only idea that can satisfy human society. Human pride and societal piety can only be secure in a democratic set-up. If the democratic is not directionless and indisciplined, it can be the best system in the world. It is definitely the best system in the world. What needs to be done is to remove the defects and deficiencies so that it becomes better and more logical.

In India the situations of struggle are created on many topics without proper thinking and discussion that a dangerous situation is created for national unity and secularism. India is the only country in the world that generates doubts on the National language and national values. We are the only country in the world that is always sensitive towards its development. Small countries have found success in making their languages prestigious on an international level. Despite a limited number of people speaking German, Spanish, French, Korean, Japanese and Latin languages, these are international languages. Contrary to this, Hindi that is spoken by about 100 crore Indians has not been able to gain the expected respect.

In order to unite the country efforts should be made to develop and popularize Hindi all over the country. It should not be developed in a way that it undermines the language of a particular state. If we can give English more importance than our own language, then why can't we give it to our mother tongue, Hindi. Especially in the North-East and Southern States, an environment against Hindi is created. This has no logic.

Hindi strikes a natural balance between all Indian regional languages and all Indian citizens feel proud and a sense of belonging when they speak and read it. Hindi as a language that is uniting the country should be strengthened and the work of acceptance of Hindi in a non-Hindi speaking state like Meghalaya should be made stronger. Since the past few years the misbelief among various non-Hindi speaking States is being erased that Hindi is being forcefully imposed on them. Hindi is capable and eligible of gradually displacing English as the language that can unite the entire country.

From far away South to the States of the North-East a special fondness for Hindi seems to be making its presence felt. Most of the youth from the Northeastern States feel that if they have to enter the mainstream of the country, they have to learn Hindi. Although some selfish interests try to implement narrow politics in the name of opposition to Hindi. Stalin was not happy with the names of cities being written in Hindi on the milestones on the National Highway. This shows the short sighted behavior of Indian citizens that they easily put foreign culture and foreign actors on a pedestal, but feel difficult to give respect to fundamental Indian symbols.

When the Raj Sabha parliamentarian from Mizoram, Ronald Sapa Talau, raised the question of the bad plight of Hindi in his State, many people were pleasantly surprised because the normal thinking is that Hindi is not liked in Mizoram. He told the House that since the month of March about 1300 Hindi teachers were on a hunger strike, because they had not got their salaries for the past 10 months and their services had also been terminated since February. Teachers are kept on contract in every State and these teachers are forever grappling with the government, but the case of Mizoram is different because these were Hindi teachers. In order to increase the acceptance of Hindi and teach them the language, it is important for these teachers to be there.

If we look at Mizoram's history we will see that since the past two decades, the State has been in the grip of a violent campaign. Not only do the Mizoram protesters spread false propaganda against Hindi, but consider it to be the root cause of all their problems. Mizoram's left-wingers feel that the spread of Hindi will lead to a spread of Hinduism also. In such a situation they try to create an environment of hatred by connecting Hindi and Hindus. This is not something new. The efforts of linking Hindi and Hindus have been made directly after independence. During a discussion in Parliament, Ramdhari Singh Dinkar had vehemently opposed the statement of his fellow parliamentarian, Frank Anthony, who has said that Hindi is the language of Hinduism. Removing all doubts about Hindi, Dinkarji had said, "Hindi is not a language of a narrow mindset, but that of liberalism. Hindi is as tolerant and liberal a language as India is a tolerant country."

There is no doubt that India is again trying to get back its pride. India is making strides in a lot of fields. Despite many problems and obstacles, we are not stopping. Various social norms and obstacles try and stop us, but we are slowly moving ahead on the path of becoming a capable and developed country. The obstacles that pose a problem are many, such as- corruption, social inequality, security, domestic violence, etc.

Politics should be value-based

The root of India's myriad problems is its directionless politics. We will have to change this situation. Politics should be for people's welfare. Man's spiritual welfare cannot be kept away from it. How can the sole objective of politics be to rule?

The political viewpoints that have been popular in the world since the past few decades have not made adequate preparations for man's progress in the direction of moral values, ideals and spiritual development. Politics has been made into a technique and the values in it have got lost.

In India, many scholars and wise men have stressed on the need for politics to be value based. The popular political models of governance seem to be inspired by capitalism, socialism and communism. In reality, none of these concepts is holistic. The opinion of scholars like Deendayal Upadhyay has been such political ideas were brought into use without testing the practical form of man. As a result, these thoughts became an essential part of exploitation and struggle. These political principles considered men as mere physical bodies that wanted to consume and presented their debate. These ideas have made men the slaves of money and consumerism. Considering men as merely physical bodies is insulting the basic human values and his supremacy. Man can have certain needs, but calling him a slave to these physical needs will be to negate the truth.

Many intellectual thinkers have considered physical needs as necessary and considered them as important from a practical perspective. Although it is a practical truth, it is not an absolute truth. The ideal form of the best democracy can be achieved on the basis of a felling of co-operation and balance. Dwelling on the organization of the Indian state Jayprakash Narayan had said that actual democracy is not real, because the people never govern directly. It is the rule of the special people chosen by the people. Contrary to this, according to Deendayal Upadhyay, nobody is special. Everybody has been provided recognition as equal factors in a system. Each person's benefit is inherent in everybody's collective welfare, it is this idea that can validate Indian democracy.

The understanding that every society has towards human life and power, accordingly it thinks of a model for good governance. For the proper administration of the Indian state the makers of the Constitution have dwelled on the ideal form of governance since the Vedic rishis to the modern thinkers. The geographical situation of every country, its social and cultural values are unique and they cannot be violated by the government. India is also a unique country, in which the governing system can be run properly while experiencing mutual goodwill and unity.

Many great political thinkers have worked for creating the best and well developed administrative system by making good use of Indian resources which is based on the welfare of every person. Thinkers like Pandit Deendayal Upadhyay had stressed on the need for nation building by displaying patient behavior. Deendayal Upadhyay's Singular Human Philosophy is truly based on he best feelings of balance in society, affection and mutual welfare. His thoughts were deeply connected to elemental and moral dimensions. He is the representative of the basic tradition of India, in which religion is a form of good morals and good behavior. This idea of religion was not merely for the other life. It was an ideal for living well in this life itself. These principles were not merely theoretical for Deendayal Upadhayay, but he abided by these principles in his practical life also.

The philosophy of Singular Humanity guides us on how the questions of the State's system and political sphere are connected to our behavior and daily life. Politics and morality are mutually related. In Western Philosophy this is made clear in Plato's 'Republic', Aristotle's 'Economic Ethics' and Mahatma Gandhi's 'Hind Swaraj'. Morality is connected to personal gains, but the determination of personal welfare stems from social welfare only. Similarly, Political science keeps the objective of social welfare, but an ideal state system cannot be formed by ignoring personal welfare. Integrated humanity is a philosophy of the micro and the macro being mutually complementary. The relationship between a person and society is animate. It is not a relationship between bricks and houses. Society is a public creation, in which the relationship between a person and the State is the same as that of a body and living cells. With this outlook there can be no clash between the good of the person and the good of society.

Today, Indian society needs to become united and organized in all spheres. We are often not able to unite as a nation and this is the main reason for our failures. If India is not able to become a capable and able country even after having all the eligibility, the main reason is that we are not able to function as a united country. Indian society has remained divided and parted due to historical reasons. Foreign powers have taken advantage of the situation and have looted us for thousands of years. The society has to become aware and united so that such a situation does not arise again. If all of us can be imbued with a feeling of cooperation, the biggest of works can be completed and accomplished with greater ease.

There is no doubt that the government and its agencies also need to change and improve, but as citizens we too have a responsibility towards the society and the country. The first step to cooperation is to develop a feeling of partnership with harmony. This feeling also gives rise to a feeling of oneness and sensitivity in society. The society that has a feeling of oneness and cooperation can face any challenge. Collectivity changes a society much more easily, and when society changes the country automatically changes.

Today, if important campaigns such as the 'Cleanliness campaign', 'Education for all', 'Environment protection' or 'Beti Padhao' campaigns are not moving ahead with the expected speed, it is no doubt that the reason is a lack of collectivism. The effort to remove this can bring about a big change because already there are many people who are quietly carrying forward such campaigns. Why don't all of us become a part of these campaigns? When this country belongs to all of us, then why is the work of developing and beautifying it left to only some people?

Behaviour, not merely the planning, builds the nation

There is no doubt that every work of nation building cannot be done at the government level. Governments do not do everything. And this is also not new that making laws is not everything. The main thing is the implementation of the laws. And this happens when every citizen thinks that it is his duty to follow the laws. The Indian society seems to be united on those occasions when there is some emergency situation or a situation of imminent war. Recently the country seemed to be united at the time of revolutionary decisions like Demonetization and GST. The question is why does the Indian society know how to become united only in times of emergencies? When the task of nation building should happen in society during peace–time, then where does the unity disappear?

Various types of bad habits have entered the Indian society due to historical reasons. The work of dividing society into various castes and classes has been deliberately done. This divided India into numerous parts and it became a slave to foreign invaders for thousands of years. All Indians should forget their differences and selfish interests and consider the good of the country as their own good. We should make efforts to bring the resourceless section of society to the forefront in all spheres of life.

Today the country is moving forward in this direction. For this process to continue the deprived and neglected section of society needs to be empowered in an economic and social manner. Their talent and participation should be utilized in nation building. An extensive campaign needs to be started against social discrimination and inequality in the Hindu society. Such efforts are being made and they always yield good results. It is the result of the increasing awareness against the social evils in the Hindu society that the 'Dalit Indian Chamber of Commerce & Industry', i.e, 'DICCI', has more than 5000 small and big Dalit industrialists as its members.

The government has started various initiatives like 'Stand-Up India' to give upcoming entrepreneurs their creative assistance to various projects. And directions have been issued to more than one and a quarter lakh branches of Public Sector banks to provide financial assistance to entrepreneurs from the scheduled castes and scheduled tribes. This creative change is what we required today. Efforts like these can improve the future of thousands of neglected youth and make it secure.

Talent can take birth in any place and at any time. Every year we see so many poor and rural talented people make the country proud in various examinations and competitions. From all the school examinations conducted in the country to the prestigious 'All India Civil Services Examination', thousands of poor children and those deprived of opportunities in life leaving the mark of their talent. If such talent gets proper opportunities they can do a lot of work for the benefit of the society and country. It is everybody's responsibility that they get the security and opportunity.

We often hear news that despite a lack of resources and opportunities many Indian talents have surprised the entire society with their displays and results. Recently in Bharatpur (Rajasthan), the son of a laborer scored 98.2% marks in the 12th class State Board examination. Similarly in Bhilwara also in Rajasthan, a boy from a poor family was chosen in the IIT-JEE. This change is not restricted to a few cases. In the last many years, the neglected youth of society has been doing creative work for the betterment of society.

Efforts have been made on the subject of social equality for thousands of years. Several questions can be raised on the speed and appropriate results of these. It is obvious that such change cannot be brought about by making Constitutional arrangements and symbolic laws. For this we need to make revolutionary mental changes and start social campaigns on a war footing. Before Ambedkar, the credit for preparing the ground for the welfare of Dalits goes to the founder of the Arya Samaj, Swami Dayanand, Lala Lajpat Rai, Swami Shraddhananad, Veer Sawarkar, King of Vadodara-Sayaji Rao Gaekwad, Master Atmaram Amritsari, Lala Gangaram Sareekhe and other great men.

There has been the extraordinary contribution of social workers who have come from high class families with progressive ideas for working towards social equality. Swami Dayanand was the first person to give the right of reading the 'Vedas', of doing 'Yagyas', doing the 'Gaytri Paath', and of sitting and eating together. Swami Shraddhanand is called the originator of the word Dalit. Before that 'Dalits' were called untouchables. Swamiji had given his resignation letter to the Congress because it was not taking the matter of Dalit uplftment with seriousness. Not only this, he has established the system of 'Kangdi Gurukul' in order to see that everyone got the same education.

Veer Sawarkar established the 'Patit Paavan' temple while migrating to Ratnagiri and helped the Dalits gain access to temples, but he also appointed Dalit priests. The king of Vadodara, Gaekwad gave a scholarship to Dr. Ambedkar and sent him abroad to get an education. There is no doubt that Dr. Ambedkar could not have done the work of upliftement of Dalits without an education. Master Atmaram was the great soul who made arrangements for the education of Dalit children in Gujarat. With the viewpoint of social equality many organizations have been working in India for the past many decades. The greatest and most intensive of these has been that of the Rashtriy Swayam Sevak Sangh.

Harmony brings unity

Organizations like the 'Rashtriy Swayam Sewak Sangh' have made an incomparable contribution towards establishing social harmony in the country. Even today some people do not accept these efforts because of their narrow mentality. The reality is that at the time of establishment of the Sangh, the first convenor of the Sangh, Dr. Hedgeware had this firm belief that the society could not become strong and united without establishing social equality in it. It was his belief that it was because of this lack of unity that foreign invaders had looted India without any worries. He knew that the Indian society did not have the capability to stop him, because a very small section had the rights to pick up arms and fight wars because of the caste system of Hindu society.

The foreign invaders had also made an analysis that despite such serious situations the Indian soldiers did not even have their meals together because of their narrow mentality and unscientific caste mentality. After getting this type of information, which foreign invader would not want to have the desire of exploiting this weakness of a rich country like India? From Mohammad Bin Kasim to Mahmud Ghaznavi, Moahmmad Gaori, Khilji, Babar, SherShah Suri and the east India Company, the sequence of looting and spoiling India continued unabated. It was the Sangh's clear vision that just political freedom was not enough for India's welfare. If India was to be developed as a capable nation, there was a need to develop a sense of love for the nation and an overall development of its character. For this the citizens would have to dedicate themselves to the cause of national and social welfare. An India that is capable can be developed by sacrificing personal interests and a disciplined behavior.

We should accept the determined loyalty of the Sangh towards social equality. Since its inception there has been this trend among the workers that they do not use any word in their names that gives an identity into their castes. Even the Swayam Sewaks who have been working together since so many years in organizing the various activities and programs of the Sangh are not keen to know the caste identities of their fellow Sewaks and nor do display any type of doubt or dilemma in their behavior and work. It is an astonishing fact that the feelings and behavior that the Sangh absorbed about 100 years ago, has not yet been understood by other political, religious and social organizations.

Evaluating one part of one's body as inferior and addressing it as Dalit puts a question mark on our own intelligence, spirituality, socialism and creativity. Actually the people who are at the bottom of the development scale, need their self-confidence to be brought up. Such self-confidence cannot be injected by people with immediate selfish interests and now can this be done by the medium of political power. This work has to be done by the society itself and is done by social and religious leadership.

There have been campaigns against Untouchability and Inequality in many parts of India. For historical reasons the disease of caste discrimination has been present in the Indian society like a cancer. In Kerala, the Alva and Pulya, etc castes are considered untouchables. The 'Pulyas' were considered untouchables to the extent that if they bought vegetables, etc from the market, it was to be kept outside the house and when a Muslim or Christian used to touch it then it used to be taken inside the house. On seeing this, Swami Vivekanand had given the term of 'Pagalkhana' to Kerala. Such people did not have access to spiritual centers and temples also. In such a situation the expansion of the Hindu society and 'Sanatan' Culture got gradually destroyed. Over a period of time, a great social reformer and thinker, Shri Narayan, made his entry into the same Alva society, who did not arise feelings of animosity among the rest of the community and established independent temples, gave them Sanskrit education and there was such a surge of self confidence amongst the people that they left the rest of the societies behind in the race of economic progress.

Similarly, in Punjab the Jats were considered as lowly. Guru Nanak Dev and those after him helped them gain respect in the society and today they are seen as an enterprising community not only in India, but all over the world. The Ramghariya community of Punjab has played an important role in the industrialization of Punjab. Dr. Baba Saheb Ambedkar had faced very adverse circumstances but did not let them prevail over him. On the basis of his talent and hard work he gave a novel and logical form to the Indian Constitutional System and methods. Even today the entire country expresses its gratitude towards his intellectual talent and great works of reform.

The deprived sections of the Hindu society should be definitely given the desired respect because this is that section that did not give up on its cultural awareness and traditions despite the many challenges. Even in the era of radical Islamic rule this section did not change its religion despite the various incentives. They were subjected to much torture for this. They were forced to do hard and inferior type of work. They were ready to undergo anything, but were not ready to convert their religion. Nobody knows how and when this bitter truth of history was forgotten with the passage of time.

The warriors of the Hindu society that was defeated by foreign invaders were given the choice of either accepting Islam or cleaning the toilets of the Mughals. Many people of the so called high classes accepted Islam, but the religious loyalty of these warriors was so strong that they accepted the cleaning the latrines, but did not sacrifice their religion. Whereas they should have been given utmost respect in society, the Hindu society left them at the lowest level. This can only be called the unfortunate and short–sighted behavior of Indian society.

Now, there is no doubt that caste discrimination and social inequality are the cancers of Indian society. Till the time this cancer is there this nation in the form of the body will not benefit. A strict law should be made and this cancer should be treated. Bitter medicines will not suffice now. If we want freedom from this cancer, we will have to perform surgery. The viruses are eating into the organs of the body. There are such people in the Indian society who want to keep this social cancer close to their chest for their own personal interests. Caste discrimination can be beneficial for some people, but at the end it is as harmful for society as one cannot differentiate between good and bad terrorism, because at the end the loss is to the human society.

Some powerful castes and political groups want to keep this caste discrimination alive at any cost. Luckily these castes are also politically powerful and are against any change. A great concept like 'reservation' has also been ridiculed by various political parties. Instead of making proper use of it, it is being grossly misused.

Even those castes have started demanding reservations that have faced social ostracization. Today reservation has become a political tool. This has weakened the political and constitutional campaign to remove social inequality.

The objective behind reservation is that of social justice. It is to give those weak sections of society a participation in the employment, educative and economic development of the society who have been deprived of it for centuries. This is not being done properly in the present system. The other castes that are included in the 'Other Backward Classes' also need to be given a taste of social justice and efforts should be made in this direction as soon as possible. Maintaining the Status Quo would be social injustice for these deprived castes. At this point the concept of sub-castes comes to the fore, i.e, making of different sub-classes under the class of reservation on different basis.

Some sub-castes can be created under the reservation limit on the basis of social, educational, economic and geographical conditions. In this context, Andhra Pradesh, Bihar, Mahrashtra, Tamil Nadu, Puducherry, etc. are examples. In these states 2-3 sub classes have been made under the reservation limit on the basis of backward castes. In Andhra Pradesh 5 sub castes have been made under the Reservation Limit. The ultimate objective of reservation is to bring the lowest castes of society into the mainstream.

Drugs making the country hollow

Indian citizens are found to be victims of many types of behavioral defects and bad qualities. In the entire world, Indians are the most addicted to drugs. And it is in India that the most quantities of alcohol, hemp, opium, beedi, tobacco, cigarette, smack and other drugs are used. Indian society is becoming passive and is falling into a situation of destruction. The habit of taking drugs is extremely harmful for any society, despite the government and society alerting people in an extensive manner crores of Indians are addicted to drugs in some form or the other. They are slaves to their habits. Even after knowing that their habit is taking them to economic, physical, mental and social destruction, they cannot control themselves.

We all know that smoking is injurious to health and it can cause a life threatening disease like cancer. Strict warnings are given on all types of intoxicating substances, but people are slaves to their own habits and are not ready to shed them. Not only do people ignore the warnings, they also make fun of them. The biggest human resource of our country, our youth, are coming under the net of drugs. States like Punjab and Haryana are facing various problems because of drugs.

Most of the crimes that take place in Indian society are also done under the influence of drugs. In crimes like violence and rape, drugs are the biggest factor. The society is wasting its energy because of this habit and the number of people in hospitals is increasing day by day. There is social damage because of the diseases and deaths caused by drugs. One can see such youth inhaling cigarette smoke at every nook and corner in villages and cities, and smashing their hopes and dreams to dust. Those who have not yet crossed the threshold of youth are wavering under the influence of drugs.

The youth of those people is at stake on whose shoulders the future of the country rests. What will happen to that future on which hang a thousand dreams and wishes. Their dream seems to be crashing. At an age where they should be having pens and books in their hands, they are playing with cigarettes, 'paan' and 'gutkha'. These days, youth are also getting addicted to hemp, cannabis, cocaine, smack and bhang. Earlier, alcohol was an enjoyment for the rich class. Now various cheap variants of alcohol have become a part of the daily life of ordinary people. Addiction to drugs is a disease that is quickly devouring us and our society.

It is unfortunate that the youth power that should have been used in the creation of the country has reached a powerless state and has become diseased under the influence of drugs. It is affecting adolescents and small children too.

At an age when children should be studying in schools they are becoming addicted to drugs. They are becoming victims by sometimes emulating others, or falling into bad company, or in trying to show that they are matured than what they really are.

The need today is to have strict laws that totally forbid the use of drugs. If drugs are totally banned, the country can be saved from many types of diseases, immoral acts, crimes, violence and anarchy. We should not forget that the business of drugs is a major part of the agenda of anti-national powers. In the border areas of India, these powers are making drugs freely available to the local youth and are pushing them towards their death. These youth who become addicted to drugs are easily lured into anti social and anti-national activities. It is surprising that despite it being such a dangerous problem, no political or social consensus is being able to be formed for its eradication.

The business of drugs is anti social and anti national. No excuse or logic can make a case for the existence of drugs in society. Drugs are making the young generation hollow. This generation that has become a victim of physical, mental and behavioral passivity and morbidity cannot be capable of creating a capable country. It will be possible only when the society stands up in a determined manner against the bad habit of drugs.

8

Service leads to the formation of Society

For the creation of a better society and a well-organized administrative system a feeling of service and dedication should be present in the citizens. Moral values are transmitted in society only through the medium of service. Good will, equality, and compassion can be established in society only through service. Service does not merely mean receiving, but it also means dedicating oneself to one's idol and devote himself to his object of desire with all of one's energy. Its result or remuneration is also not materialistic, instead it is spiritual and heavenly. The ultimate elements that give us eternal pleasure and spiritual experience cannot be compared with any physical substance. It is incomparable and invaluable. The experience of the greatest element is possible only in the cells of the heart that provide eternal pleasure. The truth is that no materialistic happiness or worldly achievement can take the place of pleasure.

Work that is done in relation to one's source of livelihood and by remaining in one's work sphere are also mediums of service. The remuneration from this appears as physical and creates a momentary happiness and the next moment its attainment gives rise to dissatisfaction, disappointment, regret, wavering of the mind, disinterest and a feeling of injustice and negative feelings. Earning one's livelihood is work that is done for progress or with expectation of reward, in which more than dedication, respect and service, there is a feeling of selfishness, the desperate desire for materialistic gains and curiosity. The remuneration received by earning one's livelihood makes possible the fulfillment of various social and personal needs.

The process of earning one's livelihood should not be limited to mere physical achievements. If it is made the medium of social and spiritual progress, then each of our works will become pure and worthy of emulation. While we are on this earth, which is our work place, livelihood, is important. The fulfillment of earthly requirements needs money and resources. We should work hard and accumulate resources and riches according to our needs, but proper use of these resources will be made only when they are extensively used for the betterment of people. The Indian constitution has also defined a feeling of service as necessary qualities for the system, administration and citizens.

As soon as the feeling of service develops, the most ordinary looking task appears sacred and effective. Even in the Indian Constitution, the quality of service has been defined to be a necessary quality for citizens, the governance system, and the administration. The fundamental principle of the Constitution and the Directive principles of State Policy and fundamental duties of citizens provide acceptance to the feeling of service. There is no doubt that the administration should be replete with Constitutional values and the great feeling of people's service. Administrative values should never be sacrificed at the altar of political agendas. Whether there is the government in power is of any ideology, the governance has to be impartial and work according to the system provided by the Constitution.

A government servant and administrative worker should be like Arjun and always keep his eyes fixed on the objective. He should hold an impartial view towards gains and losses, political views and keep himself occupied with the welfare of the country.

A government servant should do his work diligently and do work that is result-oriented. In the past few years, complaints have started coming that the administration is being politicized. Political parties put pressure on the administrative machinery and try to push forward their political agendas. Many times the administrative machinery deviates from its main objectives and national responsibilities.

Today, many administrative thinkers believe that in various states the officials have become so politicized that from their postings to their promotions, discrimination is visible everywhere. The negative aspect is also visible on the work of the bureaucracy. Their postings and promotions are decided on the basis of personal interests. This happens particularly during elections. The Election Commission gives orders for the transfers of some dubious officials, but it does not make any difference, because the people holding power have already foreseen the situation and made arrangements accordingly. Generally the politicization of officers is done more by those political parties whose only objective is to get hold of power any which way. They do not have much dedication towards good governance, benefit of the country an social welfare. Many times government officials and workers also forget their responsibilities and try and appease them for their own selfish interests.

Along with the criticism and evaluation of the government and the administration, it is necessary that we understand their challenges also. Without understanding the complexities that face the government machinery, we cannot evaluate them in a justifiable manner. In this age of mental tensions, the responsibilities and the duties of the government are constantly increasing. In a vast country like India, government officials have to face many tensions in order to fulfill the expectations of the people. It affects their mental and physical health in an adverse manner. The tiredness of constant work and the weakening of mental and physical capabilities in the police administration leads people to keep a negative attitude towards them.

The ordinary people make various allegations at the police and administration, but hardly ever think about their difficult working conditions. The situations that are turning the police into an unpopular workforce are those that are turning them into machines. These situations should be properly investigated because without proper working conditions the police cannot be made an efficient and sensitive force. Governance discharges its duties at the level of officialdom in its vast sphere of work. In this manner they carry out their governance and constitutional works, and manage the population and control it. If improper use of force is applied it creates anger and resentment among the people.

Today, the society and the circumstances are changing. The citizens are aware and have access to information. They know how to complain against laxity in order and provision of services. In this age of information technology people know how to raise their voice against problems and place them before the higher levels of authority. In such a case the expectations from the government machinery increase. For the fulfillment of these expectations, the government machinery does not have the required resources, capabilities and work force. Without decreasing the difference between the shortage of resources and the provision of services, criticizing the government machinery would be doing injustice to it.

In the modern technological age, technology is changing very quickly. There is pressure on everybody to stay updated. The police administration cannot be an exception to it. It has also got to change. Actually, it should be the first one to change, because it has the constitutional responsibility to organize and control the society. That is its main challenge. Today, we have come very far from the medieval thought, where corporal punishment was acceptable in its extreme form. With the changing times, corporal punishment is now the last resort and that too when it is completely and properly justified. No doubt that this is correct and is the recognition of a cultured society.

The responsibility for a well organized and disciplined governance mechanism does not lie only on the government and the administration. The role of society and the citizens is of utmost importance. For the creation of an organized society and well-organized democracy, the making of a citizenry that knows its responsibilities is very important. If a citizen is disciplined and responsible towards the country and loyal towards the society, then only an ideal society and a democratic nation can be possible. Whatever work we do, we should remember that this entire country and society belongs to us. No selfish interest or need that is personal should be above the welfare of the country and the society. As soon as this feeling is born in us, our every work starts to be beneficial, worth emulating and a source of guidance for our society, country and a healthy democracy. Even if we have to sacrifice some personal benefits for the extensive benefit of society, we should never hesitate to do it. In reality our supreme gain lies in the welfare of the country and the society.

Our view-point in the form of a citizen should be holistic. 'This entire country and its environment belongs to me and I have to constantly look after its organization', should be our relentless goal. If a person throws the garbage of his house outside and thinks that he has cleaned his house, it will be called his ignorance. He should remember that the other person who has the same narrow-minded attitude would also do the same thing and throw out his garbage outside the house. It is this type of thinking that has harmed a country like India too much. We are not able to inspire our citizens to think in a liberal manner. This work has to become the responsibility of the family and society.

The youngsters and young generation should be given these values from the beginning that whatever they do should not be adverse for the country, society or other citizens. If the citizens start giving their contribution towards nation building in an aware and disciplined manner, the work of the government and the administration will become easier. In the absence of citizens' awareness, even the government and administration cannot do anything.

It is very clear that the end objective of public service and the administration is people's service. Besides this, there are no other expectations from them.

It is very important that the Indian Public Administration should not waver from its basic objective of service. The feeling of service is the main quality of a human being's life. Without it, we cannot imagine the creation of a healthy and meaningful society. In reality the concept of service is at the center of Indian culture, civilization, tradition and spirituality. Indian citizens should imbibe this quality and throw themselves into the task of nation and society building. Especially the youth need to show this quality.

The maximum ability for service and people's welfare is found in the youth. The youth power should be properly used in the work of building the society and the nation. The personality of the youth can be honed and changed through the medium of service. When service is the only objective of life, the mind becomes concentrated. This makes our works purposeful and we get long lasting and permanent happiness. We can expand our sense of service and put an end to the fear, disappointment, anger and bad habits in our lives.

There is no doubt that the biggest problem of today's young people is that they are not focused. Because they are not focused, they are slaves of their sense organs and their minds. Their lives become deficient in Yoga, and the feeling of service. He has become robot-like. The entire focus of his life is to obtain good marks in examinations, somehow manage to find a source of livelihood and then go about amassing as many materialistic products as possible. Since his memory is becoming short-lived, he is unable to understand the meaning of human life. The youth of today have made the small things of life big and give secondary topics the utmost importance. This is happening because of immaturity of thought and short sightedness.

Today's youth has started believing that merely by buying products and appliances his respect in society goes up and his life becomes meaningful. This is a wrong notion. A man's respect depends upon his personality and his good qualities. For thousands of years our objective has been to take inspiration from the lives of the greatest people and to imbibe the qualities from their personalities.

What has happened to today's society? We do not even have the time to think of the direction in which our lives are headed. All twenty-four hours of the day our minds are under pressure of work, the noise of transport and the rings of mobile phones. These things have caused a lot of harm to our mental and physical health. Are our policy makers, society and intellectuals able to see any cure for this problem?

In order to give the right direction to our lives, we will ourselves have to come forward. The youth need to pay special attention to this. The youth can get help to open up their blocked minds with the help of certain processes, meditation and yoga. In order to get rid themselves of negativity they will have to take responsibility for themselves and will have to ensure that their minds are not full of false ideas and notions.

Society is moving away from labour

It is unfortunate that modern Indian society does not give the required acceptance to loyalty and hard work. We want to get the maximum results by doing less or no work. Because of vested interests, we constantly want to take advantage of the facilities that we have got as inheritance. We want to take everything from society, but we have nothing to give to the society and the country. Because of selfishness and greed we do not want to work, but keep on using the facilities that have been bestowed on us.

The lack of hard work and eligibility helps breed injustice and a situation of status quo prevails. New talents do not get proper opportunities. This causes an increase of injustice, indiscipline, anarchy and violence in the society. We are seeing this situation in almost all walks of life. Nepotism has been a big problem in India because since ancient times we have not given importance to hard work and dedication towards work.

Successful and prosperous people often become comfortable in their positions and do not want to leave their advantageous positions in any way. Their children also become a part of this process–whether willingly or unwillingly. This nepotism can be seen in India in all fields of life, businesses, industries, etc. From politics to cinema, sports to art and culture, from literature to media, from law to medicine- we have been seeing a few families at the top in all these fields. If the members of a family are talented and eligible, then they become acceptable, but even if they do not show a talent for that particular field, they are not ready to leave and in this situation they are definitely not doing justice to the society and other citizens.

It is not necessary that a person get historical success just because of his family roots and nepotism. In a vast country like India the only benefit that he gets is that he does not have to struggle for a stable career. In the field of Indian cinema, there has been the supremacy of a few families. Members of the Kapoor, Chopra, Mukherjee, Bacchan, Irani, etc, families have been easily making places for themselves in the film industry. Although they might not have been successful, they easily get entry in films and the work that they want to do. In reality, this is a universal phenomenon.

This nepotism seems to be in a most explosive situation in the political sphere. It proves to be an easy and powerful career for the members of the family. Many times these members are ineligible, but manage to get a foothold on the strength of various constitutional arrangements and strong background. Even if they are not elected, they maintain their political standing by being nominated. The Kennedy, Bush, Gandhi, Yadav, Scindia, Bhutto and Sharif families have also made the political careers of their next generations easier. In the fields of arts and culture, sports etc, one also needs to be eligible besides being inheritors of a legacy. In these spheres short cuts don't work.

If one sees in cricket, the members of the families of Amarnath, Gavaskar and Manjrekar could achieve something only on the basis of their talents. Even after average performances in one-day matches they could not retain their positions in the team. Rohan Gavaskar could never play a test match. Just the name of Gavaskar was not enough for him to spread his radiance at the international level. In some professions nepotism and inheritance work while in others it does not. Nepotism can be accepted to the extent that it does not do the work of stopping eligible and new talents from entering any field.

The young generation of the country should definitely get their due opportunities. Our extensive national interests and social values cannot be neglected just so that some people and families are benefitted. Unfortunately just some people and families have got a monopoly over India's assets and resources. This situation is not just and acceptable. In India the top 1% of citizens hold the wealth and resources of 90% of the other population. This puts an obstacle in the path of development of the country. Hard work should be given importance and the bad tendencies of nepotism should be curbed and restricted.

Satymev Jayte (Truth always wins)

A man should definitely be a follower of truth. If truth puts a value on someone's prayers, humility, forgiveness and goodness, untruths do the work of turning a person's simplicity to be his compulsions. The lies that are told out of selfishness are revealed before truth. In truth, there is an in increase in gratitude. Falsehood flourishes because of ingratitude. Truth follows lies till the time the real face does not come forward. Lies make all efforts to make truth waver and fall down, but surrenders when it is disappointed. Truth is a true feeling, whereas lies is the foundation of cheating and deceit. Truth gives prominence due to resolution. Lies fall down on getting an alternate route. Truth increases respect. Lies consider excuses to be character and repents afterwards. Lies call the other person's good behavior sin and his own crime as good behavior. Lies make people criticize you, whereas truth diminishes criticism. Truth takes a vow to protect his saviour till the last breath, whereas lies do not stop at disrespecting the saviour. Lies always believes what other people say and harbors myths, whereas truth believes after something has passed the test of gold.

There is no doubt that truth is the one and only ideal of life. Truth is the best value, Godliness and the ideal human value. Truth is the only best method of obtaining success. Any success or progress that has been obtained by deviating from the right path, can never be real success or progress. Falsehood destroys the spiritual base of a person. This misleads the society. It is basically a negative tendency. Falsehood and lies have always been used in order to make the bad seem good. Falsehood is not long lasting. It cannot remain stable for a long time. In order to hide one falsehood, one has to eventually tell many lies. In order to support one falsehood, we need the support of a thousand lies.

Our entire peace and progress are inherent in following the path of truth. Falsehoods are used to hide the truth. While truth is a great beneficial, falsehood is utterly selfish. Truth does not cross the boundary of decency, whereas lies are without morality. Relationships that are based on truth are strong, permanent and long lasting. Lies destroy the soul of relationships. By making the excuse of being busy, lies cheat and deceive. Truth takes out time and bares its soul. Lies are bad values and the route to one's downfall. If one gets success by lying once, one gets into the habit of lying. Less knowledge nurtures lies. Those who hide the truth make the simple person feel shy and take him for a ride. As soon as the water level rises above the nose, the difference between truth and lies is revealed. Truth considers guests as Gods and invites them, whereas lies make some excuse and do not have the courage to stay. Lies are ultimately a vehicle for betrayal, downfall and bad values.

In reality, it is not enough to consider truth as a fundamental quality. It should become the basic foundation of our daily behavior and entire thoughts. By adopting the truth the work of improving our personal life and bettering the society can be achieved. Mankind hides the truth in order to avoid punishment. Today, hiding the truth is considered mature behavior and practicality. The truth is that whatever shortcomings are there in this world are secondary. If there is one major fault, it is 'lies'. It is lies that are a fundamental fault. All the other practical faults are just its offshoots. Well- behaved people who pursue spiritual meditation should definitely follow the truth. Truth should never be hidden at all.

Amongst all the good qualities that a person acquires, truth is the best quality. The search for truth is the one and only meditation and hard work. In ancient Indian philosophy and spirituality we have seen that since ancient times, numerous great people have dedicated their entire lives in search of this truth. The work of sowing of the seeds of truth in a person should be made from childhood itself. This is that value by which the society can be rid of all types of injustice, inequality, violence, anarchy and selfishness.

If we accept the truth, we will surely come to realize what is good and what is bad for society. What is the truth and what is not the truth. Children should be encouraged to speak the truth. This is not something that is immature and impractical, but is a great quality. Not only in the house and in schools, but in moral science and spirituality also there should be stress on the truth because it pays a lot.

Today, we cannot even imagine that a person can be totally truthful. The type of life that we are leading now, it is even difficult to imagine that so many great men have taken form on this earth, who established a life based on truth. Despite many hardships, struggles and challenges, they did not leave the path of truth. It is also surprising how these great men faced so many problems, but still did not waver from the path of truth. They did not even utter a single false or wrong word in their lives.

This self declared journey of the so-called development of human life has made us paupers at the behavioural and meditative level. We have made economic progress, but we have gone backward as regards to moral values and the ideals of life. Today, human life despite having all sorts of amenities and a consumerist life-style, is in the grip of many vices and negative thinking. This is causing tension and disharmony in the society.

Many such negative thoughts are manifesting themselves in human life today that keep surfacing in our minds. We need to be free of both these fears–external and internal. Although it is not easy; but constant meditation, regular practice and good company can help us to attain this great state. No doubt, it is a very difficult task. Most of us do not even come to know of which thing we are fearful. The reason for most of our fears is our selfishness and our endless desires. We are afraid of what will happen in the future. Not only are we fearful of the present, but also of the future. We keep thinking that we might come in the grip of some disease, or something bad might happen to us.

Actually, fear is closely connected to happiness and luxuries. For most of the people today, physical products and amenities and luxuries have the utmost importance. We want to procure these products and amenities at any cost. We are always fearful that these amenities and luxuries might be taken away from us. We even experience these products at the level of our mind and body. In this manner, thoughts are the originators of the happiness or fear that we feel.

Thoughts are extremely important for man and society. This is the only device that we have that creates a feeling of fear or courage in our minds. These thoughts are the reaction of some memories that we have nurtured due to some experience, knowledge or traditions. Memory is the result of time. We react with this as the background. The process is based on thoughts. Dependence on things, persons and thoughts gives rise to fear. The main reason for dependence on others is ignorance. We are not able to understand our powers and spiritual capabilities.

Fear actually deviates our life from the good path. It makes us come in the grip of doubts and diseases. Because of this doubt we deviate from the right path and become slaves to materialistic thoughts. Because of this our life becomes a victim of doubts and becomes direction less. This uncertainty becomes an obstacle in transmitting our thoughts and in understanding things. We can start looking for the root cause of fear by being aware towards our self. Gradually we will come to know the cause of our fear. We are able to understand only the surface fear. Fear is often connected to past experiences. We should try and find a solution to the reasons for fear by doing a proper evaluation of our past thoughts and experiences.

Today, man's life is becoming somewhat direction less. Today, we give more importance to gossip in our life. Our attention is not on the real qualities and objectives of life. We have considered Materialistic achievements as the "one's all". We do not fight shy of throwing all moral values out of the window while pursuing our materialistic ends. This is not a good situation. If we keep on using this hard obtained human body just for getting sensory pleasures and materialistic happiness, it will be an insult to the great life that we have been given in the form of human beings. We are caught up in this vicious circle because we do not have the real knowledge. The biggest requirement that we have today is of discipline and good company.

The will power of human being grows stronger in the contact of spiritualism and yoga. Due to strong will power, one can always be a winner and win over all the fears and sadness. Till the time we are not full of confidence and do not become aware and make efforts for obtaining the real purpose of human life, nothing happy or permanent will occur in our life. We have to change ourselves. Actually, there is nothing outside in this entire creation or society. This entire country, society and creation is as it is as we ourselves are. It is not possible that we harbor any number of bad traits and we keep on demanding a better and more organized country and society. If there is something that needs to be changed; it is we ourselves, and our outlook. The moment we start changing ourselves, that moment this society, country and the entire world will start changing accordingly and as time progresses.

❍❍❍